# Caribbean Desserts

# Caribbean Desserts

by

## John DeMers

The Crossing Press
Freedom, CA 95019

Cover and text design by AnneMarie Arnold.
Cover illustration and interior illustrations by AnneMarie Arnold.

Printed in the U.S.A.

---

**Library of Congress Cataloging-in-Publication-Data**

DeMers, John, 1952-
      Caribbean desserts / by John DeMers.
             p.   cm.
      Includes index.
      ISBN 0-89594-558-4             ISBN 0-89594-557-6 (pbk.)
      1. Desserts--Caribbean Area.  2. Cookery, Caribbean.  I. Title.
TX773.D363  1992
641.8'6'09729--dc20
                                                                    92-11267
                                                                    CIP

To Sandra,

Sara, Michael, Amanda Claire

and Tessa

☼

Each of you

is the loveliest of islands,

shimmering in the bluest of

warm seas.

# Contents

# Pies & Tarts, 75

Passion Fruit Pie ❀ Groundnut Molasses Pie
Lime Pie ❀ Chocolate Rum Pie ❀ St. Kitts Coconut Pie
Sweet Potato Pie ❀ Cream Cheese and Rum Pie ❀ Cho-Cho Pie
Papaya Pie ❀ Bajan Pineapple Pie ❀ Coconut Cream Pie
Plantain Tarts ❀ Guava Pie ❀ Prune Tart
Currant Tartlets ❀ Jamaican Orange Tart ❀ Pie Crust

# Puddings & Pones, 97

Rice Pudding with Guava Sauce ❀ Pitch Lake Pudding
Sweet Potato Pudding ❀ Pineapple Bread Pudding
Puddin di Coco ❀ Tembleque ❀ Forgotten Pudding
Crema di Sorsaka ❀ Cassava Pone ❀ Cho-Cho Pudding
Flan de Queso ❀ Breadfruit Pudding ❀ Pineapple Rice Pudding
Sweet Fungi ❀ Cornmeal Pone with Coconut Topping
Carrot Pudding ❀ Christmas Pudding ❀ Coconut Milk

# Chilled Delights, 121

Trifle ❀ Banana Whip ❀ Daiquiri Soufflé
Rum-Raisin Soufflé ❀ Coffee Bombe ❀ Island Parfaits ❀ Papaya Delight
Pineapple Royal ❀ Passion Fruit Mousse ❀ Martinique Coffee Mousse
Mousse a L'Ananas ❀ Mango-Papaya Sorbet ❀ Nutmeg Ice Cream

# Coffees & Other Beverages, 137

Café Aruba ❀ Jamaican Coffee ❀ Coffee Grog
Cancun Café ❀ Flaming Rum Coffee ❀ Hot Buttered Rum
Batido Cubano ❀ Coquito ❀ Sorrel Drink ❀ Ginger Beer

# Sources of Caribbean Foods, 145

*Caribbean desserts* are an open window into the Caribbean soul—a rich and bountiful entity where one finds suffering alongside sunshine, austerity alongside bounty, passion alongside contentedness. One also finds in the spectrum of island desserts the full impact of the region's centuries of ethnic mixing.

As I returned to the islands to assemble this collection of sweets, not only did discoveries jump out at me as they never had before, but the scribbled recipes gathered from 20 years of Caribbean travel seemed to call me back for a fresh look. It was like spotting someone incredibly good-looking and discovering that here was the girl or boy who sat across from you unnoticed in the second grade. It was a matter of learning to see beauty with newer, truer eyes.

Contemplating at length the scribbled recipes themselves, I remembered the many hands that had done the scribbling—hands that belonged to bent dark bodies beneath white hair and rainbow-hued bandanas. Every hand belonged to a smile, and every smile came with a warm, patient voice that almost invariably called me "Honey." These were friends of friends on island after island, sometimes the grandmothers of friends of friends. Many had passed on, I now realized, and nearly all were beyond any hope of tracking down. In some cases, even their names had been lost, though their faces never will be. Yet their scribbles remained. These yellowing scraps of paper were not so much my possession as they were my muse, my authority, and, in the end, my commission to write this book.

# Sweets from the Melting Pot

The same ingredients that today make certain desserts taste Caribbean are the very ones that formed a cluster of lovely islands into a recognizable region. Sugar, spices, tropical fruits, and rum made for the successive scramble of empires that is Caribbean history. We don't know exactly what lured the original Indians to the islands; but we do know that once the courts of Europe heard of this New World bounty, they climbed all over each other claiming islands as their own.

The history of the Caribbean is written in the desserts themselves, each a tale of human aspiration and suffering. When we taste the real Caribbean in its desserts, we must admire the nameless and numberless cooks who expressed so much of themselves in this single, sweet legacy.

It is my conviction from 20 years of island travel that the Caribbean is a nation in the making (I mean socially more than politically), a people in the making, born of many races and languages, many shades of color and intent. Today, this group of people is born of many islands, some still colonial and some quite independent. It's hard to visit even the tamest island without glimpsing something bigger, something wilder, something passionately human just below its carefully polished surface. That something has been in formation since long before the first European eyes gazed into the mirror of these waters and knew they were seeing their future.

It is reasonably certain that the Arawak Indians who abandoned the lowlands of South America for the Caribbean islands brought their cooking with them. The beginning of what we call barbecue was one of their contributions, as were dishes using corn, sweet potatoes, beans, callaloo, guavas, pineapples, and papayas. The Arawaks pounded cassava, whipped it into batter, and fried it into a delicious bread they called bammy. They turned whatever meat and vegetables they could find into a soup called pepper pot. And they perfected a method of spicing and spit-roasting wild pig that today fascinates us as jerky.

Europeans first saw the Caribbean in the 1490s, in a series of "discoveries" by Christopher Columbus. It took nearly a century for the Spanish to become serious about colonization, but once they did the peace-loving Arawaks' days were numbered. They were forced to teach their new overlords all they knew about island life, and then were eliminated from the Caribbean scene. I'd like to think their legacy remains in some foods, as well as in the islands' intrinsic tolerance and preference for peace.

Though the Spanish brought many of their cooking techniques with them—frying and dishes made with beans and peas—they made their greatest contribution to Caribbean desserts with what they planted: bananas, plantains, sugarcane, lemons, limes, Seville and Valencia oranges, coconuts, tamarind, ginger, date palms, pomegranates, and figs. And they supplemented these gifts from the Old World with careful selections from the New, including guinep and naseberry.

The Spanish experience in the Caribbean proved inspirational, particularly to other European powers wishing to possess this strategic shipping zone. Looking for places to grow sugar and coffee, the French took over Martinique, Guadeloupe, Haiti, and several other islands. To this day, there are travelers who prefer the French West Indies to all other corners of the Caribbean—travelers who embrace the French West Indies' savory blend of "la cuisine classique" with "la cuisine créole."

Both the Dutch and the Danish were major players in the great Caribbean land-grab throughout the 1600s. Explorers from the Netherlands planted their flag on Aruba, Curacao, and Bonaire, bringing a sea chest full of recipes with them. Among the most intriguing is the pungent rijsttafel, a food festival of 40 dishes imported not just from Holland but all the way from Dutch Indonesia. The Danish maintained three of Columbus' favorite ports for 250 years. Eventually, the United States picked up St. Thomas, St. Croix, and St. John and dubbed them the U.S. Virgin Islands. Despite American control since 1917, natives of these islands still love their "Danish table"— a bountiful buffet known everywhere else as smorgasbord.

Counted among the most adaptable colonists were the Portuguese Jews who arrived in the Caribbean along with the first Spaniards. They specialized in confections—especially caramel cakes made with imported sesame seed. They hired native women to sing of their wares on the streets, starting a rich market tradition that at its best sounds lovelier than opera to me.

Then there were the English. It's impossible to imagine the Caribbean without them. They were active in the region for 300 years, laying the foundations of what would become the region's most secure democracies. Jamaica and Barbados (along with the Bahamas and Bermuda outside the Caribbean proper) are genteel testimonials to the good the English could do when they set their minds to it. Other testimonials include the new colors they added to every islander's culinary palate: breadfruit from the *Bounty's* infamous Captain Bligh, otaheite apple, mango, rose apple, mandarin orange, turmeric, black pepper, and world-famous Blue Mountain coffee. It was none other than the English who introduced rum. And it was none other than the English who left a near-addiction to cakes, pies, and tarts along with Christmas puddings and Easter buns. Seasonal desserts devoured in the English islands tell the time of year as accurately as any calendar.

Of all the legacies that shape today's Caribbean, there is none more tragic, more enduring, or more profound than that of the Africans who came in chains. As soon as the Spaniards eliminated the Arawaks, they turned to Africa for the strong backs needed to bring in their empire's harvest. West Africa was the scene of a quite different harvest—first from the Ashanti and Fanti tribes, later from the Yoruba and Ibo.

Despite all odds and indeed against the tireless efforts of their masters, slaves prospered in the Caribbean. Long before their peaceful emancipation, they had planted gardens around their huts to grow okra and yam from their homeland, along with callaloo, corn, pumpkin, ackee, and coffee. By the close of the eighteenth century, they were selling the surplus from their crops to buy what they could not grow, a list headed by meat and salt fish. Along the road to freedom, the Africans left their mark on every piece of the Caribbean, from the rhythms of reggae to the graceful lines of their wood carvings. They left their mark on cooking as well—providing a smattering of purely African recipes plus a library full of soulful "touches" added to every other colonial cuisine.

If slavery provided the backbone of Caribbean economy and culture, then freedom set the stage for the immigration that made it the richest melting pot of all. When the freed slaves declared they wanted nothing more to do with plantations, landowners launched a desperate effort to lure cheap labor from abroad. This labor was never cheap enough for a system built on getting it free, so the plantation system was doomed. Yet the Germans and Irish arrived nonetheless, followed by large numbers of immigrants from Asia and the Middle East. Laborers from India contributed unexpected spiciness to everything they touched, including the curries the English had already learned to love. The Chinese brought their tradition of stir-fry and the ongoing romance of rice—themes picked up and made their own by the Syrians and Lebanese who followed.

Eventually, into our own day, a new style of immigrant makes his way to the Caribbean—in a sense, a new style of buccaneer. Entrepreneurs from the United States, lured by the promise of paradise, are broadening Caribbean cuisine once again to include foods such as cheeseburgers and pizza. It's easy to bemoan these additions, seeing them as diluting the "true" flavor of the islands. Yet the Caribbean has always been in flux, created by people lured by opportunity or need, bringing with them their memories, contributing a new energy and a new vision.

In cuisine, as in all things, change is disturbing. Yet in the Caribbean, change has always been the status quo, sowing seeds from the past in hopes of harvesting the future.

## Flavors of the Islands

*Sweet, spicy, and spiked*—these describe Caribbean desserts in terms of their main ingredients. For although the island sweet tooth is legendary, it is ever tied to the same spices that ignite Caribbean savory dishes and the same rum that powers nearly every Caribbean drink.

Although this basic understanding will get you into the island kitchen, it will not protect you from constant surprise. Whether it's the numberless combinations of sweet and spicy in desserts you thought you already knew, or the deft way island cooks adjust all ingredients by instinct, you'll find there's much to learn. The fact is, each time you think a dessert is merely a New World execution of an old Old World standard, the island cook will hit you between the eyes with a pinch or a splash you're certain to find nowhere else. Don't be lulled by familiarity; you'll miss the better part of the fun.

What follows are the briefest descriptions of the main ingredients island cooks use to make their desserts sweet, spicy, and, when appropriate, spiked.

## Sweet

So much sweetness is supplied by the rainbow of tropical fruits in the Caribbean that sugar at times seems almost an afterthought. So in addition to the familiar granulated, brown, and confectioners' sugars, your sweetening strategies should include the following gifts of nature.

*Pineapple*— On many islands this fruit is known simply as "pine." It is thought to have originated in Central America and the Caribbean. In addition to being good eaten all by itself, pineapple is versatile. It finds its way into numerous savory dishes as well as an impressive proportion of the desserts collected in these pages.

*Coconut* — So often paired with pineapple, coconut is a member of the palm family. It hails from Malaysia and has taken to the western tropics with gusto. Yielding fruit the year around, coconut caresses island desserts in a number of different forms: as water or "jelly" from the green fruit, or as grated meat from the mature. It also supplies coconut milk and sweetened coconut cream.

*Banana* — In the Caribbean, bananas are eaten both green (in cooked dishes) and ripe (in dishes or all by themselves). Mashed or creamed, fried or flambeed, the banana is omnipresent in island pies, cakes, and sweet breads.

*Oranges* — Caribbean oranges are plentiful—and far more varied than visitors from the north are likely to expect. Generally, they can be divided into two categories: bitter or sweet. Historians tell us the rather acidic Valencia and Seville came from Spain and found a permanent place in drinks and marmalades. The islands developed several other varieties over the centuries, including ortanique, navel, and ugli.

*Grapefruit* — Many experts claim that grapefruit originated in Jamaica, a place where it was well established before any other of the world's citrus-growing regions heard of it. Though some believe that the name describes the sight of grapefruit hanging in clusters, it is generally thought to reflect a perceived similarity in the flavor of grapefruit and grapes.

*Mango* — This fruit was actually discovered in the shadow of the Himalayas, yet it is now known as the "peach of the tropics." From the high mountain regions, it was successfully transplanted to warmer climates: India, China, Latin America, and the Caribbean. Island dessert cooks feel that the best varieties of mango are the Bombay, East Indian, St. Julian, and Hayden.

*Papaya* — Pawpaw is the name you'll most likely hear for this fruit in the kitchens of the Caribbean. Papaya has its origins in South America but today is island food beyond argument. With its bright orange color when ripe and its slightly bland flavor, papaya works well when blended with more sharply flavored tropical fruits. It also turns up often as a simple drink sweetened with sugar or the ever-popular sweetened condensed milk.

*Guava* — This is one of the few tropical fruits native to the Caribbean, and as such islanders make use of it as often as they can. It's everywhere in the Caribbean, growing outside many cooks' kitchen windows, and is commonly used in jellies, preserves, fruit cocktails, wines, and desserts. Cooks can often be caught munching on the fruit while cooking something completely different!

*Lemons and Limes* — Limes began to be cultivated extensively when they were identified as both a preservative and as a cure for the scurvy afflicting the British Navy. Lemons and limes are grown widely in the islands and used in an immense variety of ways: with chicken and fish, as well as in beverages, cakes, pies, and preserves.

*Soursop* — This spiny dark green fruit, native to the American tropics, is known usually as guanabana in the Spanish islands and corossol in the French. In the States, it is often available as juice in cans or as frozen pulp in Latin American markets. Soursop is excellent in drinks, ices, and sherbets.

*Tamarind* — Condiments, candies, and beverages most often benefit from the acidic brown pulp of this tropical seed pod. West Indian markets often feature the packaged pulp; the nectar is even more widely available in cans under its easily recognizable Spanish name, tamarindo.

*Starfruit* — Native to the islands of the Greater Antilles, this green or purple fruit—also known as star apple, carambola, and kaimet—is now being grown in the United States. When cut crosswise, starfuit has a star-shaped arrangement of pulp and seeds. It makes an eye-catching dessert garnish and turns up in the beautiful Jamaican dessert called Matrimony.

*Passion Fruit* — Although this fruit is especially popular in Caribbean drinks, its juice is much appreciated in ice cream, mousse, and sorbet—not to mention the latest innovative sauces. The fruit—long, green yellow, and hard-shelled—reveals when opened a mass of seeds surrounded by fleshy pulp.

*Cashew* — Though best known for its seed, or nut, cashew is a fruit native to the American tropics that has spread in cultivation around the globe. This pear-shaped fruit is slightly astringent in flavor, but islanders love it as a cooling drink or as a highly perfumed jam.

 Spicy

Considering the abundance of spices available and the ever-renewing interest supplied by wave upon wave of immigrants, I suppose it was inevitable that the Caribbean develop a preference for highly spiced food. Yet whether we're speaking of fiery soups and meat dishes or of spice-driven desserts, it's a mistake to conclude that this scenario rules out subtlety. Quite the contrary. Island cooks can't always tell you what they're doing or why; but their often-quirky techniques produce wonderful results.

Since the focus here is on desserts, we need not talk specifically of fresh herbs such as Caribbean thyme or of widely important chile peppers such as Scotch bonnet. Here instead is a cook's tour of the spices that make the Caribbean sweet tooth a complex affair indeed.

Allspice — In the Caribbean, allspice is known primarily as pimento (as distinguished from pimiento—the red sweet pepper stuffed into olives). Cuba grows some allspice; all the rest hails from Jamaica. Though the English love allspice in savory pickles and marinades, they also pioneered its use in sweet breads and spice cakes.

Ginger — In 1527 ginger was introduced to the Caribbean by the Spaniards from the Far East. It has been cultivated in the islands for domestic use and export ever since. Available fresh as ginger root and dried as ground powder, it is used in puddings, cakes, candies, and ginger beer.

Cinnamon — This spice was introduced to the Caribbean from Ceylon in the 1700s. Today, there's nary a country market in the islands that doesn't feature little tied-up bundles of cinnamon sticks and leaves. It is used in puddings, porridges, and other sweets, as well as in drinks and liqueurs.

Nutmeg — Caribbean cooks protest the fact that nearly all nutmeg sold in the United States is preground, insisting that it's much better to purchase the whole nutmeg and grate it as the need arises. Nutmeg is the inner kernel of a fruit, and decidedly more flavorful when freshly grated. It is used primarily in cakes, puddings, and creamy drinks.

𝓜𝓪𝓬𝓮— Nutmeg's netlike covering is mace. It starts out a lovely pink but evolves to brown during the drying process. Mace seldom stands alone, turning up most often in conjunction with nutmeg and cinnamon to spice porridges and drinks.

# Spiked

𝓡𝓾𝓶 𝓹𝓵𝓪𝔂𝓼 𝓪 𝓭𝓮𝓬𝓲𝓼𝓲𝓿𝓮 𝓻𝓸𝓵𝓮 in giving island desserts a unique personality. It is readily available in the Caribbean, since it's a by-product of sugar. Brandies and cognacs are far more expensive. For the longest time, in fact, colonists insisted that rum was a poor, lower-class substitute for the spirits enjoyed back in Europe. Now, with improved distillation and dramatically increased variety, the finest Caribbean rums are found in public and private bars around the world.

It is popularly believed that the word rum is derived (you might even say distilled) from rumbustious and rumbullion, both old English words meaning uproar. But more sober souls insist that the word rum is related to the botanical name for sugarcane (Saccharum officinarum), perhaps shortened in deference to those enjoying it in bulk. Either way, just about anybody in the civilized world can join in the chorus of an exceedingly uncivilized song and have an uproarious good time:

> Fifteen men on a dead man's chest
> Yo ho ho and a bottle of rum
> Drink and the devil had done for the rest
> Yo ho ho and a bottle of rum.

𝓡𝓾𝓶—the fermented, distilled, and aged by-product of molasses, which itself is a by-product of sugarcane—has been a part of Caribbean life and lore since the English introduced it in the 1600s. Virtually every island is proud of its own style of rum-making, and of course the islanders will assure you their native rum is the best.

I've toured enough Caribbean distilleries in my time to have pounded the process into my otherwise nontechnical brain. Special pumps press clarified and heated extracts of sugar into centrifuges. The molasses left after all crystallizable sugar is removed is then distilled with water and fermented with yeast—one day for light rum, up to 12 days for dark. The yeast uses up all the sugar and dies happy.

Actually, many parts of the world produce rum, including the former Soviet Union, Malaysia, and, yes, the United States. Yet these products tend to be relegated to domestic use, whereas the Caribbean's rums are deemed worthy of export. Generally, light rums are preferred on such Spanish-speaking islands as Cuba and Puerto Rico; dark rums find their strongest support on such English-speaking islands as Jamaica and Barbados. The French make rum (they call it "rhum") directly from cane syrup on Haiti and Martinique.

Whether it's light rum empowering a citrus sorbet, dark rum glazing a dense chocolate cake, or high-octane "151" flaming a pan of pineapple, rum is and ever will be the buccaneer spirit of the Caribbean.

# Street Sweets

$\mathcal{I}$'m really showing my hand in this category, and I trust you'll forgive my near-ridiculous enthusiasm. I've always loved the foods found in marketplaces and on street corners everywhere in the world. So it is that with Caribbean desserts, not only do we find some of the loveliest markets and streets on earth but some of the neatest sweets you can eat on your feet. See what I mean? The tastes are as contagious as the rhythms and rhymes!

Cookies, naturally enough, are a type of dessert that enlivens this dessert category—and islanders adore cookies. But just when you think you can pronounce the names all too easily, well, along come totoes, frituras, gizadas, soenchi, and something called tie-a-leaf, when it isn't known by its West African name of dokono.

On the streets, in the marketplaces, along the waterfronts of islands across the Caribbean, you can get almost anything to eat. From soup to nuts, as they say. But let's face it, the islanders are just like us. They can't quite figure out why anybody would dig into green beans or spinach when there are chocolate chip-coconut rum cookies right around the corner.

# Curacao Butter Cookies

These delightful cookie squares take their name not from the famous orange liqueur produced on the island but from the island itself. In the language of the Netherlands Antilles, they are known simply as botercoek.

1/2 pound unsalted butter, softened
1/2 cup sugar
1/2 teaspoon vanilla extract
1 1/2 cups flour
1/4 teaspoon salt

Preheat the oven to 350 degrees F. In a large bowl cream the butter with the sugar and vanilla extract until the mixture is light and fluffy. Combine the flour with the salt, then sift into the butter mixture 1/2 cup at a time, beating well after each addition. Scoop the dough onto the center of a large ungreased baking sheet. With a metal spatula or table knife, spread into a 9-inch square about 1/2 inch thick.

Bake on the center rack of the oven until firm to the touch and golden brown, about 35 minutes. Remove the pan from the oven and cut the "cookie" into 1 1/2-inch squares. Let the squares cool on a wire rack before serving.

Yield: about 3 dozen cookies.

George Washington was introduced to the pineapple during a trip to Barbados in 1751. The man who would later command the Continental army was then accompanying his illness-weakened brother to a warm climate to recuperate. After listing in his diary all the tropical fruits he was served, Washington noted, "None pleases my taste as do's the pine."

# Citrus Crisps

*I* picked up the idea for these super-citrusy nut cookies on the streets of Cancun. As it turned out, they were terrific snacks to take to the beach. The orange zest and extract in this recipe can be replaced by lemon or lime according to your preference.

3/4 cup unsalted butter
1/4 cup confectioners' sugar
4 tablespoons grated orange zest
1/4 teaspoon orange extract
1 cup flour
1/2 cup cornstarch
1/2 teaspoon salt
1 cup chopped toasted walnuts or pecans

In a large bowl cream together the butter, confectioners' sugar, zest, and extract until light and fluffy. Combine the flour, cornstarch, and salt and gradually stir into the butter mixture. Thoroughly mix in the nuts, then roll the dough in waxed paper to form a log. Chill in the refrigerator until firm, about 2 hours.

Preheat the oven to 375 degrees F. Slice the chilled log into 1/4-inch-thick slices and place 2 inches apart on an ungreased baking sheet. Bake until brown around the edges, about 10 minutes. Let cool on a wire rack before serving.

Yield: about 2 dozen cookies.

# Coconut Drops

*C*oconut drop cookies are popular on every Caribbean island. This particular recipe—without a doubt my favorite—hails from the French portion of St. Martin. It couldn't be any simpler, or any better.

1/4 cup unsalted butter
1 cup sugar
1 cup grated unsweetened coconut
2 eggs
1 teaspoon vanilla extract
1 cup milk
1 cup flour
1/2 teaspoon baking powder
1/2 teaspoon ground cinnamon
1/8 teaspoon salt

Preheat the oven to 350 degrees F. Lightly grease a baking sheet and set aside. In a large bowl blend the butter with the sugar until creamy, then beat in the coconut, eggs, vanilla, and milk. Sift together the flour, baking powder, cinnamon, and salt. Add to the coconut mixture and blend thoroughly.

Drop about 2 tablespoons of the mixture at a time onto the prepared baking sheet. Bake until golden brown, 15 to 20 minutes. Let cool on a wire rack before serving.

Yield: about 2 dozen cookies.

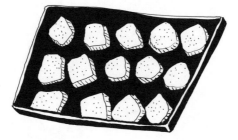

# Jamaican Rum Cookies

*I*f you're like me, you'll start eating these wonderful cookies flavored with dark rum as soon as they come out of the oven. But you will find, as many Jamaicans already know, they're even better allowed to "mellow" for a few days in an airtight container.

2 teaspooons dark rum
1/2 cup unsalted butter, softened
1 cup packed brown sugar
2 eggs
2 cups sifted cake flour
1 teaspoon baking powder
1/2 teaspoon salt
1 teaspoon ground cinnamon
1/4 teaspoon ground cloves
1/4 teaspoon freshly grated nutmeg
2 cups seedless raisins, chopped
1/2 cup unsalted peanuts or cashews, chopped

Preheat the oven to 350 degrees F. Lightly grease a baking sheet and set aside. In a large bowl cream together the rum, butter, and brown sugar until light and fluffy. Add the eggs one at a time, beating after each addition. Sift together the flour, baking powder, salt, cinnamon, cloves, and nutmeg; then add to the rum-butter mixture. Blend in the raisins and the nuts.

Drop 1 teaspoon of the mixture at a time onto the prepared baking sheet; allow for considerable spreading. Bake until brown, about 10 minutes. Be careful not to overbake. Let cool on a wire rack before serving, or store in an airtight container to improve the flavor.

Yield: 4 dozen cookies.

# Panlevi

$\mathcal{I}$t is said that each morning on Curacao, phone conversations crisscross the island to find out who is feeling a bit under the weather. These calls are followed by a flourish of panlevi baking, since these light sponge cookies are considered to be good medicine for just about anything that ails you. You'll find that they taste good as well.

4 eggs

1 cup sugar

1/4 teaspoon ground mace

1 teaspoon vanilla extract

2 1/2 cups flour

1/8 teaspoon salt

Preheat the oven to 325 degrees F. Lightly grease and flour a baking sheet and set aside. In a large bowl beat the eggs until frothy, then gradually stir in the sugar. Add the mace and the vanilla, blending thoroughly. Sift the flour with the salt, then fold into the egg mixture.

Drop the batter 1 tablespoon at a time onto the prepared baking sheet. The batter should form peaked mounds; allow space for the cookies to spread to about 2 1/2 inches in diameter. Bake until the edges are golden brown, about 20 minutes. Do not overbake; the cookies should be both crisp and chewy at the same time. Let cool on a wire rack before serving.

Yield: about 20 cookies.

# Chocolate Chip – Coconut Rum Cookies

*B*lending the traditional Latin love of chocolate (an obsession the conquistadors picked up from the Aztecs) with tropical coconut and rum, these Puerto
Rican cookies will be winners from your kitchen every time.

1 cup plus 2 tablespoons flour
1/4 teaspoon salt
1/2 teaspoon baking soda
6 tablespoons unsalted butter, softened
1/2 cup packed light brown sugar
1/4 cup granulated sugar
1 large egg, lightly beaten
3/4 teaspoon vanilla extract
3/4 teaspoon light rum
1/2 cup semisweet chocolate chips
1/2 cup grated unsweetened coconut

Preheat the oven to 375 degrees F. Lightly grease a baking sheet and set
aside. In a small bowl sift together the flour, salt, and baking soda. In a large bowl,
with an electric mixer beat the butter with the sugars until the mixture is light
and fluffy. Add the egg, vanilla, and rum and beat well. Fold in the flour mixture
followed by the chocolate chips and coconut.

Drop the mixture 1 tablespoon at a time onto the prepared baking sheet.
Bake until the edges turn golden brown, 8 to 10 minutes. Let cool on a wire rack
before serving.

Yield: 24 to 30 cookies.

# Tie-a-Leaf

You'll find this intriguing marketplace sweet from West Africa sprinkled from island to island across the Caribbean—under different names, of course. Dokono is the original Fanti tribe's name for it, though "blue drawers" seems to turn up pretty often as well. I personally believe that the name "Tie-a-Leaf" is the most Caribbean, since it's poetry in motion while revealing the basics of what goes on in the recipe.

3 cups yellow cornmeal
1/4 cup flour
1 cup sugar
1/2 cup grated unsweetened coconut
1 teaspoon ground cinnamon
1 teaspoon ground allspice
1 teaspoon salt
1 tablespoon molasses
2 tablespoons vanilla extract
2 1/2 cups Coconut Milk (see page 120)
8 banana leaves or corn husks, for tying

In a large bowl mix together the cornmeal, flour. sugar, coconut, cinnamon, allspice, and salt. In a medium bowl mix the molasses with the vanilla and Coconut Milk. Add to the flour mixture and stir briskly.

Place 1/2-cup servings of the mixture onto banana leaves or corn husks that have been boiled until pliable or onto squares of aluminum foil. Fold up the sides around the mixture and tie together with banana bark or twine. Place the sweet parcels in enough boiling water to cover and cook for 40 minutes. Let cool on a wire rack, then cut the twine and serve in the packages.

Yield: 8 servings.

# Totoes

*I*f you'd like to introduce young children to the sweet flavors of the Caribbean, you might start where most parents start in the islands themselves—parceling out these delightful snacks.

2 cups flour
2 teaspoons baking powder
1 teaspoon ground cinnamon
1/2 teaspoon freshly grated nutmeg
1/4 cup unsalted butter
1/2 cup granulated sugar
1/2 cup packed light brown sugar
1 egg, beaten
2 teaspoons vanilla extract
1/2 cup milk, or as needed

Preheat the oven to 375 degrees F. Lightly grease an 8-inch square baking pan and set aside. In a medium bowl mix together the flour, baking powder, cinnamon, and nutmeg. In a large bowl cream the butter with the sugars until fluffy, then gradually add the flour mixture.

Add the egg and the vanilla, followed by just enough of the milk to make the batter the consistency of cookie dough. Spread the batter into the prepared pan and bake until golden brown, 30 to 35 minutes. Let cool, then cut into 9 squares. Serve or store in an airtight container.

Yield: 9 squares.

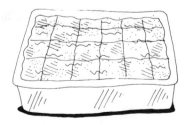

# Benye

*P*art of the fun of this spiced Caribbean doughnut is seeing how the French word beignet took on a decidedly African spelling, and wondering whether, somewhere in the past, it wasn't really the other way around. The batter is much the same as for French beignets, except for the island spice. But the benye is dropped into oil by spoonfuls, rather than being rolled out, cut, and carefully lowered. Remember, the batter must be refrigerated overnight. But the good news is it keeps for a week, so you can enjoy a batch here and a batch there if you like.

1 package (1/4 oz) active dry yeast (about 1 tablespoon)
1 1/2 cups warm water
1/2 cup sugar
1 teaspoon salt
4 teaspoons ground cinnamon
1 teaspoon ground mace
1 teaspoon freshly grated nutmeg
1/2 teaspoon ground cardamom
1/2 teaspoon ground cloves
2 tablespoons grated orange zest
2 large eggs
1 cup evaporated milk
7 cups flour
1/4 cup vegetable shortening
Vegetable oil, for deep-frying
Confectioners' sugar, for sprinkling (optional)

In a large bowl dissolve the yeast in the warm water. Add the sugar, salt, spices, orange zest, eggs, and evaporated milk. Gradually stir in about half the flour, beating with a wooden spoon until thoroughly blended. Beat in the shortening, followed by the remaining flour, working in the last of the flour with your fingers when the batter becomes too thick to stir. Cover the bowl with plastic wrap and refrigerate overnight.

Heat the oil in a deep fryer to 360 degrees F. Drop in the batter by generous spoonfuls and fry until golden brown. Turn with a slotted spoon if necessary for uniform color, then drain on paper towels. As you complete each batch, set it on a platter lined with more paper towels and place in a 200 degree F oven to keep warm. Sprinkle with confectioner's sugar, if desired, before serving.

Yield: about 5 dozen doughnuts.

Though taken for granted today, the banana was virtually unknown in the United States a century ago. A single blackened banana, left over from a vessel's food stores, would fetch a hefty price after arriving in New Orleans from Central America and being shipped north to Boston wrapped in aluminum foil. A Cape Cod sea captain named Lorenzo Baker was the first to see a market for bananas shipped from the West Indies. After 15 years of bringing them north with other cargo, Baker formed the Boston Fruit Company to do the same thing on a larger scale. His company merged with that of a railroad magnate in Costa Rica just before the turn of the century, and the United Fruit Company was born. Within two decades, bananas were making their way by refrigerated ships and railroad cars to markets all across the country.

# Frituras

This is the name given to sweet and crisp pumpkin fritters on the streets of Puerto Rico, with the words de calabaza sometimes added for those who don't know the main ingredient already.

1 cup canned pumpkin
2 eggs, beaten
1/2 cup flour
1/2 teaspoon salt
1/4 teaspoon ground cloves
1/2 teaspoon ground cinnamon
2 tablespoons sugar
Vegetable oil, for frying

In a large bowl thoroughly mix the pumpkin with the eggs. In a separate bowl sift together the remaining ingredients, then add to the pumpkin mixture and mix to form a thick batter.

Pour 2 inches of oil into a skillet and heat until hot. Drop the batter 1 tablespoon at a time into the oil and cook until brown on both sides. Drain on paper towels before serving.

Yield: about 16 fritters.

# Gizadas

Of all the sweet snacks I've sampled in the Caribbean, this is one of the simplest and best. It's almost like a tiny tartlet, except that it's tossed together with none of the care associated with classical confections.

1 cup grated unsweetened coconut
2/3 cup packed brown sugar
1/2 teaspoon freshly grated nutmeg
1 recipe Pie Crust dough (see page 96)

Preheat the oven to 375 degrees F. Grease a baking sheet and set aside. In a medium bowl mix the coconut, brown sugar, and nutmeg. Pinch off small pieces of the pie crust dough and roll out on a lightly floured surface into 3-inch circles. Pinch the edges to form a ridge, then fill with the coconut mixture.

Arrange on the prepared baking sheet and bake until golden brown, about 20 minutes. Let cool on a wire rack before serving.

Yield: 6 to 8 servings.

*In 1843 islanders in Grenada played host to an English sea captain homeward bound from the Spice Islands in the East Indies. To show his gratitude, the captain left behind a few small nutmeg trees from the East when he set sail again for England. Grenada harvested its first crop of nutmeg 15 years later. Today it produces nearly 40 percent of the world's supply.*

# Soenchi

Though sometimes known as "meringue kisses" for their resemblance to the chocolate candies of that name, these popular snacks are called soenchi in the islands of the Netherlands Antilles. The local cooks say that these confections should be lightly tinted red or green, never boldly colored. And they also advise that especially in humid climates, soenchis should be eaten at once since they absorb moisture and become sticky.

1 egg white
1 1/2 tablespoons sugar
1 drop red or green food coloring

Preheat the oven to 250 degrees F. Lightly grease a baking sheet and set aside. Beat the egg white until stiff and dry, then gradually stir in the sugar and food coloring. Drop by teaspoonfuls onto the prepared baking sheet. Place in the oven for 1 hour. Allow to cool on the baking sheet, then serve at once.

Yield: about 1 dozen soenchis.

# Sweet Potato Balls

$\mathcal{T}$hough sweet potatoes are often cooked as a savory side dish, there's no question in the Caribbean mind that the sweet potato was destined to be a dessert. This treat, its natural sweetness enhanced with coconut milk and sugar, is a terrific snack to eat while browsing through a lively island market. The boniato is the sweet potato favored in the islands. Also available is the incorrectly named but sweeter Louisiana yam—not a true yam at all.

2 pounds sweet potatoes, scrubbed
6 cups water
1 teaspoon salt
3/4 cup Coconut Milk (see page 120)
3 cups sugar
1 egg yolk
Ground cinnamon, for dusting
Whole cloves, for garnish

Cut the sweet potatoes into pieces and place with the water and salt in a large saucepan. Cover and boil over medium heat until fork-tender, about 40 minutes. Drain the potatoes, then peel and mash through a sieve into a medium bowl.

Add the Coconut Milk, sugar, and egg yolk and mix well with a wooden spoon. Pour the mixture into a heavy saucepan and bring to a rapid boil, stirring constantly. Reduce the heat to medium and cook, stirring, until the mixture separates completely from the bottom and sides of the pan. Remove from the heat and let cool slightly.

Divide the mixture into small balls. Dust them lightly with the cinnamon, garnish each with a whole clove, and serve.

Yield: 16 balls.

# Almond Candy

The almond tree is one of the loveliest landscape specimens in the entire Caribbean, inspiring poets, songwriters, and quite a few restaurateurs to trade upon its beauty. There are well-known eateries named after the almond tree on several islands. This recipe for candy built around whole almonds hails from St. Martin, where the cooks say peanuts work wonderfully too.

4 cups packed light brown sugar
1 stick cinnamon
1 cup water
1 pound whole almonds, shells and skins removed

In a large saucepan combine the brown sugar, cinnamon, and water and bring to a boil, stirring constantly until the sugar dissolves. Add the almonds; then reduce the heat and, stirring, cook until the mixture measures 250 degrees F on a candy thermometer. Remove from the heat.

Drop 1 to 2 tablespoons of the mixture at a time onto a cutting board or piece of marble dampened with water. Let the candy stand until hardened, about 1 hour. Serve, or store in an airtight container.

Yield: about 2 dozen candies.

*Caribbean limes tend to be larger and juicier than those found in other parts of the world. They are so fragrant, it's hard to imagine the "Caribbean experience" without them. They are used in numberless sauces, in dishes constructed around seafood, poultry, and vegetables, and in a nearly endless list of spectacular desserts. Oh yes, lime does go nicely with rum as well!*

# Candied Coconut

Sometimes spotted in the Caribbean as cocada, here's an intriguing sweet that's just perfect for the island palate. Stateside, we might call it "coconut brittle." Whatever you call it, try serving it the traditional way, on broken bits of coconut shell.

2 cups packed brown sugar
1 cup water
1 cup grated unsweetened coconut
Juice of 1/2 lime

Lightly butter a baking sheet and set aside. In a large saucepan combine the brown sugar and the water and simmer gently until the mixture forms a thick syrup. Heat until the temperature registers 240 degrees F on a candy thermometer, or until a bit of syrup dropped into cold water forms a soft ball. Remove the pan from the heat.

Immediately stir in the coconut and lime juice. Turn the mixture out onto the prepared baking sheet and spread to cool. Break into bite-sized pieces and serve on broken pieces of coconut shell.

Yield: about 3 cups brittle.

# Cakes

You can feel the excitement of discovering a new world when you encounter the tradition of Caribbean cakes. You can almost envision that first island cook, kneeling before an open fire, suddenly realizing that if you pour or press enough things into a pan that they hold together. Sweeten them with sugar and soak them with rum, and you just might have something fabulous when it comes away from the heat.

As you can probably tell by now, I am always excited by such "present at the creation" fantasies. Yet I'm equally excited watching an initial notion grow and twist and burst forth over the centuries as cook after cook adds his or her moment of genius. There's been a good deal of that in the long history of Caribbean cakes, with those of us who eat our way through them today as the primary beneficiaries.

As in other cultures and traditions, the name "cake" is applied with great abandon in the Caribbean. Quite rightly, we have excluded savory bits of poetic license such as "crabcakes," and we've placed island "cheesecakes" where they seem most at home, among the pies and tarts. Otherwise, cakes are open season—from the cornmeal and raisin delight known as Gateau Mais in Martinique to sweet breads and muffins turned hot from their pans. All are cakes as close as I can tell, at least more than they're anything else. And to the Caribbean way of thinking, that's enough said about that.

# Marzipan Daisy Cake

$\mathcal{R}$ich with the fruits and nuts that abound in the Mexican Caribbean, this confection was invented by nuns in a convent during the eighteenth century. It is actually a cake layered with lush custard and decorated with daisy petals formed of the almond paste.

## Marzipan
2 1/2 cups almonds, skins on
3 cups confectioners' sugar
3 egg whites
1 to 2 tablespoons unsalted butter, softened

## Custard
6 cups milk
3 sticks cinnamon
8 egg yolks
1 1/3 cups granulated sugar
1/3 cup cornstarch
1/4 cup flour
1 cup shredded unsweetened coconut
1/2 cup butter, softened
1 1/2 cups whipping cream, chilled 30 minutes in the freezer

Yellow food coloring, as needed
Confectioners' sugar, for sprinkling
Ground cinnamon, for sprinkling

To prepare the Marzipan, boil the almonds in water to cover for 10 minutes, then let them stand for 10 minutes more. Drain and peel off the skins. Dry the almonds on a baking sheet for 1 hour, then grind in a food processor or blender until fine. Add the 3 cups confectioners' sugar and blend until a thick paste is formed. Be careful not to overblend. Transfer the paste to a bowl and add the egg whites, mixing until blended. Add the 1 to 2 tablespoons butter and stir well. Set aside.

In a large saucepan over high heat, bring the milk and cinnamon sticks to a boil, then remove from the heat and let the foam subside. Repeat this process three times, then allow to cool.

In a large bowl beat the egg yolks with the granulated sugar until they turn pale yellow. Slowly blend in the cornstarch, flour, and coconut. Gradually add the cooled milk.

Simmer the mixture, stirring constantly, until it is the consistency of thick cream. Remove from the heat and stir in the 1/2 cup butter. Press buttered waxed paper onto the surface of the custard to prevent a film from forming, then refrigerate for 2 hours. Beat the cream until thick and fold it into the chilled custard.

Make the Marzipan decorations by peeling off 3-tablespoon portions of the paste and shaping daisy petals. Form 3 daisies, connecting the petals with a dab of egg white and pressing firmly with the tip of a scissors. Set the flowers on waxed paper. Pinch off 1 tablespoon Marzipan and work in the food coloring with your fingers. Shape into 3 small balls and set in the center of each flower.

To assemble the cake, grease a 9-inch round baking pan. Measure and cut a piece of waxed paper to fit the pan. Roll out a 1/8-inch-thick layer of Marzipan on the paper, then turn the Marzipan over into the pan and peel off the paper. Spread a layer of custard over the Marzipan, then make and add another layer of Marzipan. Remove the second sheet of waxed paper.

Sprinkle with the confectioners' sugar and cinnamon. Garnish with the Marzipan daisies. Refrigerate for 6 hours before serving.

Yield: 10 to 12 servings.

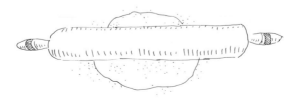

# Orange Christophene Cake

Audrey Hopkins, proprietor of the 12-room Ross Point Inn on the island of Grenada, always won her guests' gratitude by serving this local favorite. It makes extraordinary use of the chayote, called the cho-cho on many islands but the christophene on Grenada.

## Cake

1 cup flour
1 teaspoon baking powder
1/2 teaspoon baking soda
1/4 teaspoon salt
1/2 teaspoon freshly grated nutmeg
3/4 cup granulated sugar
1/2 cup vegetable oil
2 eggs
1/2 cup corn flakes cereal
1 1/2 teaspoons grated orange zest
1 teaspoon vanilla extract
1 cup shredded chayote
1/2 cup chopped walnuts or pecans

## Frosting

1 small package (3 oz) cream cheese, softened
1 tablespoon unsalted butter, softened
1/2 teaspoon grated orange zest
1 1/2 cups confectioners' sugar
1 to 2 tablespoons milk, as needed

Preheat the oven to 325 degrees F. Grease a 9-inch square baking dish and set aside. In a medium bowl combine the flour, baking powder, baking soda, salt, and nutmeg. Set aside. In another medium bowl beat the sugar, oil, and eggs until well blended. Stir in the corn flakes, orange zest, and vanilla.

Stir in the flour mixture and the grated chayote. Mix well, then spread the batter evenly in the prepared baking dish. Bake until a knife inserted in the center comes out clean, about 35 minutes. Let cool completely in the pan on a wire rack.

To prepare the frosting, in a medium bowl beat the cream cheese and the butter until fluffy. Stir in the orange zest and confectioners' sugar. Add milk as needed if the frosting is too thick to spread.

Frost the top of the cake in the pan and cut to serve.

Yield: 8 servings.

*Few people think of the Caribbean when they're staring at their morning grapefruit, yet that's exactly what they should be thinking of. Surprisingly, the fruit didn't even exist before the eighteenth century, when a British sea captain named Shaddock sailed into Jamaica bearing a large citrus tree from Polynesia. Once planted in the West Indies, the tree that would bear his name—shaddock (or pomelo)—flourished. Over time, though, a mutation appeared that seemed to be a cross between the shaddock and the sweet orange. Its skin was thinner than the Polynesian import, and its flesh was yellower and sweeter. A new fruit, the grapefruit, was born.*

# Planter's Cake

Just about every island had its planters—wealthy masters of sugar or coffee whose desserts set the civilized standards against which all more common sweets were measured. And just about every island had its own version of this planter's cake, marking a kind of evolution from pudding to confection.

1 recipe Sponge Cake (see page 52)
1/2 cup rum
1 1/2 cups unsalted butter, softened
4 1/2 cups confectioners' sugar
9 eggs, separated
1/2 cup strong brewed coffee

Cut the cake into 4 or 5 thin slices, then sprinkle each slice with the rum. Let stand until the liquid is absorbed. Cream the butter in a medium bowl, then gradually add 3 cups of the sugar and cream until the mixture is fluffy.

Add the egg yolks one at a time, beating thoroughly after each addition. Gradually beat in the coffee. In a separate bowl beat the egg whites until they are foamy. Then gradually add the remaining 1 1/2 cups sugar and beat until stiff but not dry. Fold the beaten egg whites into the butter mixture.

Reassemble the cake layers, spreading the frosting between each as well as on the top and sides. Refrigerate the cake until ready to serve.

Yield: about 10 servings.

# Port of Spain Fudge Cake

Chocolate is hardly a regular part of the traditional Caribbean dessert menu, even though the earliest chocoholics were Aztecs not too far away. This fudge cake recipe made the crossing to Trinidad from Spanish South America, and if the locals are smart they'll never let it get away.

1/4 cup vegetable shortening
1 3/4 cups sugar
2 eggs, separated
4 ounces unsweetened chocolate, melted
1 3/4 cups sifted cake flour
3 tablespoons baking powder
1/2 teaspoon salt
1 1/2 cups milk
1 teaspoon vanilla extract
1 cup chopped walnuts or pecans
Frosting of your choice, or whipped cream

Preheat the oven to 350 degrees F. Butter and flour two 9-inch square baking pans and set aside. In a large bowl cream together the shortening and 1 1/2 cups of the sugar. In a small bowl beat the egg yolks, then add the melted chocolate. Mix well.

Sift together the flour, baking powder, and salt. Add to the creamed mixture alternately with the milk. Beat until smooth, then blend in the vanilla and nuts.

In a separate bowl beat the egg whites until stiff but not dry. Gradually add the remaining 1/4 cup sugar and beat until very stiff. Fold the egg white mixture into the batter.

Pour the batter into the prepared pans. Bake until a cake tester inserted in the center comes out clean, 30 to 35 minutes. Decorate with frosting of your choice, or serve with whipped cream.

Yield: 8 to 10 servings.

# Pina Colada Cake

*I*slanders never tire of finding new ways to enjoy the flavor combinations of the pina colada. And besides, how could anyone tire of mixing pineapple, coconut, and rum? This recipe makes a generous amount of frosting, so use as much as you like to hold this wonderful cake together.

## Cake

1 1/2 cups sifted cake flour
1 1/2 cups granulated sugar
3 tablespoons baking powder
1/8 teaspoon salt
4 egg yolks
1/2 cup corn oil
1/2 cup water
1 teaspoon vanilla extract
6 egg whites, at room temperature
1/2 cup pineapple juice
1/2 cup canned sweetened coconut cream
2 tablespoons dark rum

## Frosting

1 package (16 oz) confectioners' sugar
6 tablespoons unsalted butter, at room temperature
1/4 cup whipping cream
1 egg
1 teaspoon vanilla extract
1 teaspoon almond or coconut extract
1/4 cup drained crushed pineapple
1 tablespoon dark rum
4 ounces shredded unsweetened coconut, toasted

Preheat the oven to 350 degrees F. Butter two 9-inch round cake pans and line them with parchment paper; set aside. Butter the paper. In a medium bowl sift together the flour, 1 cup of the sugar, baking powder, and salt. In a large bowl whisk the egg yolks, oil, water, and vanilla until the mixture is pale yellow. In another large bowl beat the egg whites until soft peaks form. Gradually add the remaining 1/2 cup sugar to the egg whites and continue beating until stiff but not dry. Fold the dry ingredients into the yolk mixture, then gently fold in the beaten whites.

Pour the batter into the prepared pans. Bake until the tops of the cakes are golden and spring back when touched, about 30 minutes. Invert the cakes onto wire racks to cool.

In a small bowl mix the pineapple juice, coconut cream, and rum. Brush the tops of the cooled cakes with this mixture.

To prepare the frosting, in a large bowl with an electric mixer beat the confectioners' sugar, butter, cream, egg, vanilla, and almond extract until smooth and creamy. Transfer 1 cup of the frosting to a small bowl and stir in the crushed pineapple. Add the rum to the remaining frosting.

Place 1 layer of the cake on a serving plate and spread with the pineapple frosting. Top with the second cake layer, placed smooth side up. Frost the top and sides generously with the rum frosting. Sprinkle the top with the toasted shredded coconut and serve.

Yield: 6 to 8 servings.

*Not all Caribbean fruits are equally pleasing. The jackfruit, for instance, weighs 30 to 40 pounds and at times as much as 70 pounds, which makes it a shame that it's a gross and malodorous production indeed. Although sweeter-smelling than the jackfruit, the machineel contains a milky juice that can be fatal. It was often used by the Carib Indians to poison their enemies.*

# Calypso Cake

To many first-time visitors, and indeed to many who call the Caribbean their spiritual home, calypso is the musical embodiment of the islands. This simply-prepared cake of mixed tropical fruits—a swirling carnival of orange, mango, papaya, and pineapple—might be called the Caribbean captured in confection.

1 recipe Sponge Cake (see page 52)
1 cup whipping cream
3/4 cup Caribbean coconut rum
5 cups chopped mixed fresh tropical fruit,
such as oranges, mangoes, papaya, and pineapple
Fresh mint sprigs, for garnish

Invert the cooled cake on a serving plate and, with a long serrated knife, cut a circle around the top about an inch from the outer edge and about two-thirds of the way down. To create a bowl shape in the cake, lift out wedges of cake, working from the cut circle to the center; then set the wedges, pointed end up, along the edge of the cut circle to form a fence.

When ready to serve, in a chilled medium bowl whip the cream with 1/4 cup of the coconut rum until the mixture is stiff. Fold another 1/4 cup rum into the whipped cream, then sprinkle the remaining 1/4 cup rum over the cake. Reserving 1 cup of mixed fruit for garnish, gently fold the remainder into the whipped cream. Spoon the fruit and cream into the center of the cake. Garnish with the reserved fruit and sprigs of fresh mint, and serve.

Yield: 12 to 14 servings.

# Pineapple-Lime Cake

This densely textured, moist cake is a favorite around Cancun. It doesn't rise as easily as cakes made with all-purpose flour, so if you prefer you can substitute that for the whole wheat flour in this recipe. A mix of all-purpose and whole wheat flours also works quite well.

3 cups whole wheat flour
1 teaspoon salt
1 teaspoon baking soda
1 teaspoon ground allspice
2 cups sugar
1 1/2 cups vegetable oil
3 eggs, beaten
1 can (8 oz) crushed pineapple, undrained
1 cup chopped pecans
Grated zest of 3 limes
1/4 cup lime juice

Preheat the oven to 350 degrees F. Butter and sugar the sides of a bundt pan; set aside. In a large bowl sift together the flour, salt, baking soda, allspice, and sugar. Mix the oil and eggs and add to the flour mixture. Stir in the pineapple, pecans, zest, and juice, combining thoroughly.

Pour into the prepared pan and bake until a tester inserted in the center comes out clean, 65 to 70 minutes. Remove from the oven, cover loosely with aluminum foil, and let cool in the pan before serving.

Yield: 8 to 10 servings.

# Chocolate-Glazed Soursop Cake

$\mathcal{T}$his cake, which I was served at the Hyatt Regency on St. John, is one of the few to use chocolate in an intelligent way in conjunction with soursop—one of the Caribbean's favorite fruits. Soursop puree is available canned in Latin and West Indian markets. Fresh papaya puree also works beautifully in this recipe.

## Cake
2 cups soursop puree
1 1/2 cups unsalted butter, softened
1/2 cup packed brown sugar
1/3 cup honey
2 eggs
3 cups flour
2 teaspoons baking soda
1/2 teaspoon salt
1 teaspoon ground cinnamon
1/2 teaspoon ground allspice
1/2 teaspoon freshly grated nutmeg
Sliced fresh tropical fruit, for accompaniment
Whipped cream, for accompaniment

## Chocolate Glaze
1 1/2 pounds chopped semisweet chocolate
1/4 cup granulated sugar
1 cup whipping cream

Preheat the oven to 350 degrees F. Butter and flour a large springform pan; set aside. Gently press the soursop puree through a colander to remove the seeds. In a large bowl blend the softened butter, brown sugar, and honey with an electric mixer. Blend in the eggs one at a time, scraping the sides of the bowl frequently. Thoroughly incorporate the strained soursop puree.

In another large bowl sift together the flour, baking soda, salt, cinnamon, allspice, and nutmeg, then slowly blend them into the soursop mixture. Pour the batter into the prepared pan and bake until a tester inserted in the center comes out clean, about 35 minutes. Turn the cake out onto a wire rack to cool completely.

To prepare the glaze, in a medium saucepan melt the chocolate with the granulated sugar and cream, stirring constantly to make sure the mixture does not burn.

With the cooled cake on the wire rack, pour the warm chocolate glaze over the top, making certain it covers the sides. Set the cake in the refrigerator for at least 20 minutes. Serve with sliced fresh tropical fruit and whipped cream.

Yield: 10 servings.

*No matter where you go in the islands, the coconut is a constant source of food and drink. Its "water," the almost clear liquid inside the green (immature) fruit, is sometimes easier to find than fresh water. One island explorer called it "nectar of the gods." When a coconut is still young, its meat is a fresh and fruity jelly that's perfect for eating with a spoon. The meat dries out as the fruit matures. Shredded, this white meat is what graces a thousand confections from the Bahamas to Barbados.*

# Cornmeal and Raisin Cake

Here is a glorious cake with caramel sauce from the French Caribbean island of Martinique, where it goes by the name "Gateau Maïs." Somehow, the Creole French for "Corn Cake" only begins to evoke its delights.

## Cake
1 tablespoon unsalted butter, softened,
plus 1/4 cup butter, cut into tablespoon-sized pieces
4 cups milk
1 cup golden seedless raisins
1/4 cup sugar
1 cup yellow cornmeal
2 tablespoons dark rum
1 teaspoon vanilla extract

## Caramel Sauce
1/2 cup evaporated milk
3 tablespoons unsalted butter
1 cup sugar
1/4 cup water
1/8 teaspoon cream of tartar

With a pastry brush spread the 1 tablespoon softened butter evenly over the bottom and sides of an 8-inch springform pan; set aside. In a heavy 2- or 3-quart saucepan, combine the milk, raisins, and sugar. Bring to a boil over moderate heat, stirring until the sugar dissolves. Pour the cornmeal into the boiling liquid in a slow stream, stirring constantly. Continue to stir until the mixture is thick and smooth, 2 to 3 minutes.

Remove the saucepan from the heat. Beat in the 4 tablespoons butter along with the rum and vanilla. Pour the batter into the prepared pan and spread evenly with a spatula. Refrigerate until the cake is firm, at least 2 hours.

Prepare the sauce about 30 minutes before serving. Warm the evaporated milk and butter in a small saucepan over moderate heat, stirring constantly, until small bubbles appear around the edge of the pan. Remove from the heat and set aside. In a heavy saucepan bring the sugar and water to a boil over high heat, stirring until the sugar dissolves. Stir in the cream of tartar and boil briskly over moderate heat. Tip the pan back and forth constantly until the syrup turns golden brown.

Pour in the hot milk mixture in a thin stream, stirring constantly with a large spoon until the caramel has dissolved. Remove the pan from the heat. When ready to serve, remove the sides of the cake pan and run a long metal spatula under the cake. Slide it carefully onto a large platter. Serve the sauce separately, either warm or at room temperature.

Yield: 6 servings.

*Nutmeg and mace are different parts of the same nut. As the nuts ripen, their outer pericarp splits open just enough to let the mace-covered seeds fall to the ground. The still-pliable mace is stripped away from the seeds, then dried and grated. The nutmegs are shelled and sorted by size and oil content. The majority of nutmegs are ground into powder or pressed for oil. Only the best are shipped whole to gourmet markets around the world.*

# Grenadian Spice Cake

From the Isle of Spice itself comes this cake virtually sizzling with nutmeg, cinnamon, and allspice. In Grenada, this dessert is usually served without icing, since it's as rich as a pound cake.

2 cups flour, sifted
1/2 teaspoon baking powder
1/8 teaspoon salt
1 1/2 cups sugar
1 cup unsalted butter, chilled and cut into tablespoon-sized pieces
1 1/2 teaspoons grated lime zest
1 teaspoon freshly grated nutmeg
1/2 teaspoon ground cinnamon
1/4 teaspoon ground allspice
3 large eggs, at room temperature
1/2 cup milk, at room temperature
Sliced tropical fruit, for garnish

Preheat the oven to 350 degrees F. Grease and flour a 9- by 5-inch loaf pan; set aside. Resift the 2 cups flour with the baking powder and salt. In the large bowl of an electric mixer, combine the sugar, butter, lime zest, nutmeg, cinnamon, and allspice; beat on high speed until light, about 5 minutes.

Reduce the mixer speed to medium and blend in the eggs one at a time, incorporating thoroughly. Add the sifted flour mixture, alternating with the milk and ending with the flour mixture.

Spoon the batter into the prepared pan, pressing it into the corners and smoothing the top. Bake until a tester inserted in the center comes out clean, 75 to 90 minutes. Let the cake cool upright in the pan on a wire rack for 10 minutes. Loosen the edges with a thin-bladed spatula, then turn the cake onto the rack. Let cool to room temperature. When ready to serve, garnish with slices of tropical fruit.

Yield: 6 to 8 servings.

# Bolo di Rum

On the Dutch island of Curacao, the word bolo can describe either a pudding or a cake—and it's used to describe a cookbook full of variations on both. This particular rum cake can be served with frosting, sprinkled with confectioners' sugar, or accompanied by a sauce, according to your preference. But in the Caribbean, it is traditionally served all by itself.

9 tablespoons unsalted butter, softened
2 tablespoons plus 1 1/2 cups flour
1 cup sugar
4 eggs
1/4 cup dark rum
3 tablespoons freshly squeezed lime juice, strained
1 teaspoon grated lime zest
1/2 cup yellow cornmeal
2 teaspoons baking powder

Preheat the oven to 350 degrees F. With a pastry brush spread 1 tablespoon of the butter over the bottom and sides of an 8-inch springform pan. Dust the pan with the 2 tablespoons flour and spread it evenly by tipping from side to side. Remove excess flour from the inverted pan with a sharp rap to the bottom of the pan. Set the pan aside.

Cream the remaining 8 tablespoons butter in a large bowl. Add the sugar, then with a large spoon beat and mash the mixture against the sides of the bowl until it is fluffy and light. Beat in the eggs one at a time. Add the rum, lime juice, and zest, continuing to beat until the batter is smooth.

Sift together the 1 1/2 cups flour, cornmeal, and baking powder, then add to the butter mixture 1/2 cup at a time. Beat well after each addition. Pour the batter into the prepared pan and bake until a tester inserted in the center comes out clean, about 1 hour. Let the cake cool at least 2 hours before removing the sides of the pan and serving.
Yield: 8 servings.

# Bienmesabe

In Puerto Rico this dessert is called, literally, "Tastes good to me," and I am certain you'll agree. It's actually mostly a sauce that can be poured over sponge cake or ladyfingers, so that's the way it's represented here. The Cuban version of this Spanish cake is sweeter but less rich, and is known as coquimol.

2 cups sugar
1 cup water
1 cup Coconut Milk (see page 120)
6 egg yolks
1 recipe Sponge Cake (see page 52)
or 2 dozen ladyfingers
Sherry, for sprinkling

In a medium saucepan boil the sugar and water together until they form a syrup at the thread stage. Remove from the heat. Stir in the Coconut Milk, mixing thoroughly. Beat the egg yolks and add them to the mixture. Cook over low heat, stirring constantly, until the sauce thickens. Do not let it boil.

When ready to serve, sprinkle the cake with a small amount of sherry, then pour the sauce over the top.

Yield: about 2 cups sauce; 6 to 8 servings of cake.

# Banana Loaf

Desserts and breads seem to have a closer kinship than usual in the Caribbean, where the latter often are served as the former. Breads such as this one, which blends the sweetness of ripe banana with the crunchy texture of peanuts, make a fine ending for dinner or for the afternoon tea still favored by many in Barbados and Jamaica.

1/2 cup unsalted butter
1/2 cup packed brown sugar
3 egg yolks
2 cups flour
1 teaspoon ground cloves
1 tablespoon baking powder
1/8 teaspoon salt
2 medium very ripe bananas (1 cup mashed)
1 teaspoon vanilla extract
1/2 cup chopped unsalted peanuts

Preheat the oven to 325 degrees F. Grease a 9- by 5-inch loaf pan and set aside. In a medium bowl cream the butter and brown sugar until fluffy, then add the egg yolks and mix thoroughly. In a separate bowl sift together the flour, cloves, baking powder, and salt. Combine the mashed banana and vanilla, then add this a little at a time to the egg-butter mixture, alternating with additions of the flour mixture.

Beat the batter lightly until blended, then add the peanuts; mix well. Pour into the prepared pan and bake until a cake tester inserted in the center comes out clean, about 1 hour. Let cool briefly in the pan, then transfer to a wire rack to cool completely before serving.

Yield: 6 to 8 servings.

# Caribbean Gingerbread

The English, no slackers on the subject of gingerbread anywhere in their far-flung empire, devour it with particular passion in the West Indies. It was here that they found the pungent ginger—used freshly grated in this recipe—that claimed the treat as its own.

1/2 cup molasses
1 cup sugar
1/2 cup unsalted butter
1/2 cup hot water
2 cups flour
2 teaspoons baking powder
1/2 teaspoon salt
1 teaspoon freshly grated nutmeg
2 teaspoons grated fresh ginger
1 egg, beaten

Preheat the oven to 300 degrees F. Grease a 9-inch square baking pan, line it with waxed paper, and set aside. Gently heat the molasses, sugar, and butter in a medium saucepan over low heat. Mix in the hot water and set the pan aside to let cool.

In a medium bowl sift together the flour, baking powder, salt, and nutmeg. Stir in the ginger, followed by the egg. When the molasses mixture is cool, mix in the flour mixture.

Pour into the prepared pan and bake until a tester inserted in the center comes out clean, about 1 hour. Let cool in the pan on a wire rack, then cut into squares and serve.

Yield: 9 servings.

# Easter Buns

*I*n the islands as elsewhere, memory plays a major role in deciding which foods people love. And you'd have to search long and hard for an islander who doesn't remember the warming pleasures of Easter buns. These springtime delights (brought to the Caribbean wrapped in a nursery rhyme) are indeed the English "hot cross buns"—with just the right touch of extra spice.

1 package (1/4 oz) active dry yeast (about 1 tablespoon)
1/3 cup packed brown sugar
1/2 teaspoon salt
1 teaspoon ground cinnamon
1 teaspoon freshly grated nutmeg
4 cups flour
1/4 cup unsalted butter
1 cup milk
2 eggs
1/4 cup raisins
1/4 cup dried currants
1/4 cup chopped red candied cherries
1 egg mixed with 2 tablespoons milk
1/4 cup confectioners' sugar
2 teaspoons water

Grease two 9-inch square baking pans; set aside. In a large bowl mix the yeast, brown sugar, salt, cinnamon, and nutmeg with 1 cup of the flour. Melt the butter in a small saucepan, add the milk, and heat until very warm. Add this to the flour mixture and beat until smooth. Add the eggs and 1 cup more of the flour, scraping down the sides of the bowl and beating until very smooth.

Gradually add the remaining 2 cups flour and mix until a soft dough is formed. Turn the dough onto a floured board and knead until it is smooth and elastic, about 10 minutes. Grease a large bowl. Place the dough in the bowl and turn it once to coat the surface. Cover and let rise in a warm place until doubled in bulk, about 1 hour.

Punch down the dough and add the raisins, currants, and cherries. Knead to distribute them throughout the dough. Divide the dough in two equal parts, then shape each into an 8-inch square. Cut each square into 9 pieces. Place each set of buns in a prepared pan, cover, and let rise in a warm place for 1 hour.

Preheat the oven to 375 degrees F. While it is heating, cut a cross in the top of each bun and brush lightly with the egg-milk mixture. Bake until brown, 15 to 20 minutes. Mix the confectioners' sugar and water in a small bowl. Remove the buns from the oven and frost them while they are still warm. Serve warm or at room temperature.

Yield: 18 buns.

# Banana Muffins

*I* suppose I might have discovered these banana muffins almost anywhere in the Caribbean, but I did encounter them along the lovely north coast of Puerto Rico. This recipe turns out a dozen extra-large muffins with a crunchy topping of cinnamon and sugar. Sounds like sugar and spice and everything nice to me!

2 cups flour
2 1/2 teaspoons baking powder
1/2 teaspoon salt
1/2 cup unsalted butter, softened
1 cup plus 1 tablespoon sugar
2 eggs
1 teaspoon vanilla extract
2 ripe bananas (1 1/2 cups mashed)
1/4 cup milk
1/2 teaspoon ground cinnamon

Preheat the oven to 375 degrees F. Butter 12 extra-large muffin cups; set aside. In a small bowl sift together the flour, baking powder, and salt and set aside. In a large bowl with an electric mixer set at medium speed, cream the butter with the 1 cup sugar until light and fluffy. Add the eggs one at a time, then beat in the vanilla.

In a small bowl combine the bananas with the milk. With the electric mixer on low speed, stir the flour mixture into the egg mixture alternately with the banana mixture. Stir just until combined. Spoon into the buttered muffin cups.

In a small bowl combine the remaining 1 tablespoon sugar with the cinnamon; sprinkle over the tops of the muffins. Bake until a tester inserted in the center comes out clean, about 30 minutes. Let cool in the pan for 5 minutes; serve warm.

Yield: 12 extra-large muffins.

# Sponge Cake

$\mathcal{T}$rifle (see page 122), Calypso Cake (see page 38), and a host of other Carib bean desserts are constructed around the versatile sponge cake. In case you don't already have a favorite recipe, here's mine.

3 large eggs
1/2 cup sugar
1/2 cup sifted cake flour
1/4 teaspoon salt
1/4 cup clarified butter
1/2 teaspoon vanilla extract

Preheat the oven to 350 degrees F. Grease the bottom and sides of a 9-inch round pan. Sprinkle 1 tablespoon flour into the pan and shake it around to coat the sides. Pour out any excess flour, then line the bottom with waxed paper and set the pan aside.

In the top of a double boiler over hot water, combine the eggs with the sugar. Set the double boiler over low heat, beating the mixture with a wire whisk until very thick and pale, about 15 minutes. It should fall in a thick ribbon when the whisk is lifted. Pour the mixture into a medium bowl.

Sift together the flour and salt onto a piece of waxed paper. Sprinkle one-fourth of the flour mixture over the egg-sugar mixture and fold in with a rubber spatula. Fold in the remaining flour mixture, then add the butter and vanilla about one-third at a time. Turn the batter immediately into the prepared pan and smooth the top gently with the rubber spatula.

Bake until the top of the cake springs bake when touched with your fingertip, 25 to 30 minutes. Let cool in the pan on a wire rack for 15 minutes, then turn out onto the rack. Remove the waxed paper carefully if it sticks to the cake. Let cool before serving.

Yield: one 9-inch cake.

# Fruit Specialties

𝒥 tipped you off about this chapter at the very start of this book, listing tropical fruits as one of the defining flavors of island dessert cookery. Needless to say, these sun-sweetened wonders figure in every category of Caribbean desserts. Yet they also demand a category of their own. The following sweets are distinguished either by the fact that fruit plays the dominant role or by the fact that, quite simply, they refuse to fit into any other tradition.

Some are exotic and elegant, such as the flaming crepes or the strawberries folded in "tortillas" of chocolate. Others are incredibly simple, such as the bananas baked in butter, brown sugar, and rum, or sliced fruit in the Caribbean's beloved sweetened condensed milk. Still others seem to exist only to avoid the slightest chance of predictability, a list led off by gooseberries on a stick.

Since most island cooks can create fruit desserts as easily as they can reach out and pick the freshest fruit, even listing some of their best ideas is a bit like pinning a butterfly's wings. I hope that, by sharing this list that tends to pin their wings, I can inspire you enough to unpin your own.

# Crepes Port Antonio

Though overlooked by many itineraries today, Port Antonio was actually Jamaica's first tourism center, attracting visitors by ship in the early days of this century. Later, swashbuckler Errol Flynn left his mark on Port Antonio, even if his intake of gin prevented him from recalling just where or what that mark might have been. This flaming crepe dessert reminds me of Port Antonio's elegance and grace, with a bit of its own swashbuckling character thrown in for good measure.

## Crepes
1 cup flour
1 1/2 cups unsalted butter, melted and cooled
2 eggs
2 egg yolks
1 1/2 cups milk
3 tablespoons rum, for flaming

## Orange Butter
3/4 cup unsalted butter
1/2 cup sugar
1/3 cup rum
1/4 cup grated orange zest

## Sauce
1/2 cup unsalted butter
3/4 cup sugar
2 tablespoons grated orange zest
2/3 cup orange juice
2 oranges, peeled and sectioned
1/2 cup rum

To prepare the crepe batter, in a large bowl combine the flour, melted butter, eggs, egg yolks, and 1/2 cup of the milk; beat until smooth. Beat in the remaining 1 cup milk until the mixture is blended. Cover and refrigerate for 45 minutes.

Meanwhile, prepare the Orange Butter by creaming the butter with the sugar until fluffy. Add the rum and orange zest. Beat well and set aside.

To make the sauce, in a large skillet melt the butter and stir in the sugar, orange zest, and orange juice. Cook over low heat until translucent, about 20 minutes, stirring occasionally. Add the orange sections and rum. Keep warm.

To cook the crepes, slowly heat an 8-inch skillet until a drop of water sizzles and rolls off. Brush the skillet lightly with butter before cooking each crepe. Pour in 2 tablespoons of the batter, rotating the pan quickly to spread the batter over the bottom of the skillet. Cook until the crepe is lightly browned, then flip it over and brown the other side. Turn unto a wire rack. Repeat with the remaining batter.

To serve, spread each crepe with the Orange Butter. Fold in half, then in half again, then roll jelly-roll style. When all the crepes are prepared, place them in a chafing dish or skillet and heat through over low heat. Spoon the warm sauce over the crepes. To serve, gently heat the 3 tablespoons rum in a small saucepan, ignite, and pour over the crepes. Serve flaming.

Yield: 6 to 8 servings.

*To reduce a pineapple to wedges, here's a trick or two picked up in the Caribbean. Lay the fruit on its side and grasp it firmly with one hand. With a large sharp knife, slice off both the leafy crown and the base. Stand the pineapple on its now-flat end and slice off the prickly rind in seven or eight downward strokes. Make your cuts deep enough to remove the dark "eyes." Divide the pineapple into quarters by cutting across and down, then slice the triangular pieces of core from each quarter. Lay each quarter on its side and slice into wedges. There, you've done it!*

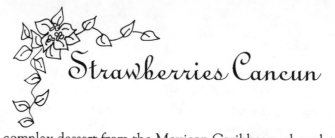

# Strawberries Cancun

In this complex dessert from the Mexican Caribbean, chocolate "tortillas" float with strawberries and a sweet cream cheese filling on a warm sabayon touched with white wine. The effort needed to prepare the tortillas will be repaid several times over when you savor this dessert.

## Chocolate Tortillas

3 eggs
3 tablespoons sugar
1/2 cup unsweetened chocolate syrup
1/2 teaspoon vanilla extract
1 tablespoon flour
5 tablespoons unsalted butter

## Cream Cheese Filling

6 ounces cream cheese
6 teaspoons sugar, plus more for sprinkling
Milk, as needed
1 pint fresh strawberries

## Sauce

4 egg yolks
1/4 cup sugar
1/2 cup white wine

Prepare the tortillas by mixing the eggs and sugar in a small bowl, then beating well. Add the chocolate syrup and vanilla, then sprinkle the flour over the top and beat to incorporate. Melt about 1/2 teaspoon of the butter in a nonstick crepe pan over medium heat. Pour in 1/4 cup batter and cook until set on top. Turn with an oiled spatula and cook briefly on the other side.

Remove the tortilla from the pan, add more butter, and repeat with the remaining batter. You should have 8 to 10 tortillas. Stack them layered with waxed paper and set aside.

Make the filling by mixing the cream cheese with the 6 teaspoons sugar in a small bowl and adding enough milk to produce the consistency of whipping cream. Set aside. Wash and trim the strawberries. Cut the large ones in half, if desired. Sprinkle them lightly with sugar.

To make the sauce, in a large metal bowl or sabayon pan over simmering water, beat the egg yolks with the sugar. Add the wine a little at a time, beating constantly as the sauce thickens. Remove from the heat when thick and fluffy. Be careful not to overcook.

When ready to serve, assemble the dessert by spooning about 1/2 cup sauce onto each dessert plate. Stack 2 tortillas atop each pool of sauce and arrange the strawberries on one half of the tortillas, reserving some for decoration. Cover the berries with the filling, then fold the tortillas in half. Spoon a bit of the sauce on top and decorate with additional strawberries. Serve immediately.

Yield: 4 to 6 servings.

# Baked Bananas

This is a simple island classic, a kind of primer in the flavor combinations that work best with the pure tropical sweetness of ripe banana.

6 large firm ripe bananas
1/2 cup dark rum
1/3 cup unsalted butter, melted
1/3 cup packed light brown sugar
3/4 teaspoon ground allspice
1/4 cup lemon juice
Vanilla ice cream, for accompaniment

Preheat the oven to 375 degrees F. Grease a 1 1/2- to 2-quart casserole dish. Peel the bananas and slice in half crosswise, then arrange them in the prepared dish.

In a small bowl combine the rum, butter, brown sugar, allspice, and lemon juice. Pour over the bananas, trying to coat them completely. Cover and bake until the bananas are easily pierced with a knife, about 20 minutes. Serve warm with vanilla ice cream.

Yield: 6 servings.

# Chobolobo

The silky texture and intriguing flavor of ripe mango take on all-new excitement in this flamed dessert discovered in Curacao. The liqueur of the same name, by the way, is made from a bitter orange called laraha that grows on the island.

2 tablespoons unsalted butter
3 tablespoons brown sugar
2 strips lime zest
1 fresh mango, peeled, seeded, and thickly sliced
2 tablespoons Curacao or other orange-flavored liqueur
1/3 cup rum
Freshly grated nutmeg, for sprinkling
Vanilla ice cream or sour cream, for accompaniment

Melt the butter in a chafing dish, then add the brown sugar and lime zest. Stir until the sugar has melted, then add the mango slices and saute until the fruit is heated through.

Remove the dish from the heat, pour in the liqueur, and shake the dish to spread it around. Add the rum and carefully ignite. When the flame has subsided, sprinkle with the nutmeg. Serve with vanilla ice cream.

Yield: 2 servings.

# Mango Fool

This particular quick-whipped dessert, incredibly popular in Jamaica, is prepared most often with pineapple. For that reason alone, I think this mango version is a bit more exotic and memorable. (I love Pineapple Fool too and make it by merely substituting that fruit for this one.)

2 cups finely chopped fresh mango
1 cup whipping cream
1 to 4 tablespoons confectioners' sugar
1 teaspoon vanilla extract

Place the chopped mango in a sieve or colander to drain for at least 10 minutes. Whip the cream in a large chilled bowl until soft peaks form. Taste the mango, then sweeten the cream as desired with confectioners' sugar. Add the vanilla to the cream and continue beating until the cream forms firm peaks when the beater is lifted from the bowl.

Separately, chill the whipped cream and the mango until it is time to serve; the cream can keep up to 1 hour covered tightly with plastic wrap. When ready to serve, fold the mango into the cream using a rubber spatula. Blend together thoroughly and spoon into chilled individual dessert bowls. Serve immediately.

Yield: 4 servings.

*Now that mangoes are offered regularly at supermarkets in the United States, someone should supply the information needed to go with them—starting with the fact that the green mango is unripe. It can be purchased green but must be left to ripen, preferably on a windowsill. It is ready when it blushes pink or yellow or, like a banana, is flecked with black or brown. Green mangoes are not totally undesired, however, since they are used in the chutney served with curry.*

# Matrimony

We think of the ingredients in a Caribbean dessert as blending together with harmony and at least a little excitement. This simple fruit dessert makes its expectation no secret, calling itself simply "Matrimony." Recent attempts to produce and market starfruit in the United States make all the ingredients readily available.

6 large fresh starfruit (carambola)
4 oranges
1 can (14 oz) sweetened condensed milk
Freshly grated nutmeg, for sprinkling
Sugar, as needed

Cut the bottoms off the starfruit less than halfway down, revealing the shape that gives the fruit its name. Scoop out the soft pulp. Pick out and discard the seeds. Peel the oranges and cut them into sections. Mix the starfruit with the orange sections, then refrigerate until ready to serve. Stir in the milk, then sweeten to taste with sugar. Sprinkle freshly grated nutmeg over the top and serve.

Yield: 6 servings.

# Blue Mountain Banana Fritters

The Blue Mountains rising above Kingston, Jamaica, produce what many consider the finest coffee in the world. I have often tramped through these mountains, collecting memories that almost invariably involve the aroma and taste of coffee. Thus I feel justified in naming these irresistible banana fritters with coffee-rum sauce for those lovely mountains.

## Sauce

1 cup sugar
1 1/2 cups strong hot brewed coffee
2 tablespoons cornstarch
3 tablespoons cold brewed coffee
2 tablespoons unsalted butter
2 tablespoons rum

## Fritters

1 cup sifted flour, plus more flour for coating
2 tablespoons baking powder
1 1/4 teaspoons salt
1/4 cup sugar
1 egg, well beaten
1/3 cup milk
2 teaspoons melted vegetable shortening
2 to 3 firm bananas

Prepare the sauce by melting the sugar in a small saucepan over medium-high heat, stirring often. Stirring constantly, slowly pour in the hot coffee. In a small bowl blend the cornstarch and the cold coffee, then stir it into the sugar-coffee mixture. Continue to cook, stirring, until the sauce boils and thickens. Remove from the heat. Add the butter and rum. Stir until the butter melts. Keep the sauce warm.

To make the fritters, sift together the 1 cup flour, baking powder, salt, and sugar. In a separate bowl combine the egg, milk, and melted shortening. Add to the flour mixture, stirring until the batter is thick and smooth.

Slice each banana into 3 or 4 equal pieces. Roll the pieces in flour, then dip in the fritter batter to coat. Fry the fritters in 2 inches of hot vegetable oil until golden brown on all sides, about 5 minutes. Drain them on a rack. Pour the sauce over the hot fritters and serve.

Yield: 4 servings.

*Many fruits have as many names as papaya, yet few have as many uses. Papaya is a natural meat tenderizer, thanks to the valuable enzyme papain, which breaks down protein tissue just as digestive juices do. Islanders have for centuries wrapped meat in papaya leaves or rubbed it with the raw young fruit to make it tender. Researchers in recent years have isolated the enzyme and adapted it into the commercial meat tenderizers used around the world.*

# Marigot Pumpkin Pancakes

Though the islands have a rich tradition of cakes, fruit-sweetened breads, and other delights baked in the oven, sometimes conditions provided only a skillet to fry up something sweet. These pumpkin pancakes from Marigot, the French capital of St. Martin, can also be made with winter squash, such as hubbard, acorn, or butternut.

1 cup flour
1/2 teaspoon baking powder
4 tablespoons sugar
1 teaspoon salt
1 teaspoon ground cinnamon
2 eggs, lightly beaten
2 cups milk
1 teaspoon vanilla extract
2 cups pureed pumpkin
Corn oil, for frying

In a large bowl sift together the flour, baking powder, sugar, salt, and cinnamon. In a separate bowl combine the eggs, milk, and vanilla, then pour into the flour mixture. Stir in the pumpkin and blend well.

Heat the corn oil in a heavy skillet. Drop the batter 2 tablespoons at a time into the skillet. Cook until golden brown on both sides, flipping each pancake once. Drain on a paper towel and serve hot.

Yield: 4 servings.

# Banana Pancakes

This recipe, also from the French West Indies, has more in common with American flapjacks or griddle cakes than the one made with pumpkin or winter squash. And with mashed ripe banana mixed into the batter, it requires no additional sweetness until you sprinkle the finished product with confectioners' sugar.

1/4 cup flour
1/2 teaspoon baking powder
1 tablespoon ground cinnamon
2 egg yolks, beaten
1/4 cup milk
1 tablespoon vanilla extract
4 ripe bananas, mashed
2 tablespoons unsalted butter, melted
2 egg whites, stiffly beaten
Confectioners' sugar, for sprinkling

In a large mixing bowl sift together the flour, baking powder, and cinnamon. In a separate bowl combine the egg yolks, milk, and vanilla, then pour into the flour mixture and stir well. Stir in the bananas and the melted butter. Fold in the egg whites and blend gently.

Let the batter settle for a few minutes. For small pancakes drop about 2 tablespoons of batter at a time on a hot, buttered griddle. Use more batter to make 4 large pancakes. Cook until both sides are golden brown. Sprinkle the pancakes with confectioners' sugar and serve immediately.

Yield: 4 servings.

# Island Fruit Supreme

$\mathcal{E}$very Caribbean cook has a favored version of this recipe, one of the simplest combinations of fresh fruits with rum and grated coconut imaginable. Here is my favorite version.

1 cup diced fresh mango
1 cup diced fresh papaya
1 cup diced fresh pineapple
1 cup sliced bananas
1/4 cup dark rum
1/4 cup grated unsweetened coconut, for garnish

In a large bowl combine the mango, papaya, pineapple, banana, and rum; blend throughly. Cover with plastic wrap and chill for at least 2 hours. Serve in dessert dishes or parfait glasses and garnish with grated coconut.

Yield: 6 to 8 servings.

# Stewed Guavas

As any island cook will tell you, guavas are a superb fruit. They can be eaten fresh or made into preserves, relishes, or some of the best chutney you'll taste anywhere. This easy sweet adds a glow to the end of any Caribbean meal.

1 cup water
1 cup sugar
6 ripe guavas, cut in half, seeds removed
1/2 stick cinnamon

In a large saucepan combine the water with the sugar. Bring to a slow boil over medium heat, stirring until the sugar dissolves. Reduce the heat and add the guavas. Break the cinnamon stick into small pieces and add; simmer for 30 minutes. Transfer the stewed guavas to a bowl. Serve in individual dessert bowls with a little of the syrup.

Yield: 6 servings.

*If you think oranges are insufficiently exotic to grace your dessert table, check out the ones sold in the islands. Few exhibit more than a passing resemblance to the brightly colored, smooth-skinned produce from Florida and California. True Caribbean oranges can as easily be bumpy as smooth, and most are as green as limes. Color is no indication of this fruit's ripeness or sweetness; these green oranges just might be the best you've ever tasted anywhere.*

# Figues Port-au-Prince

Around Port-au-Prince, the dizzyingly colorful capital of Haiti, folks love this stuffed version of the fruit we know as bananas. They call these "figues" to differentiate them from the quite different plantains (called "bananes" across the French-speaking islands), which must be cooked to be eaten. For ease of stuffing, use the largest bananas you can find.

2 tablespoons seedless raisins
1/4 cup dark rum
3 large bananas
1/4 cup freshly squeezed lemon juice
1/2 cup unsalted butter
1/2 cup confectioners' sugar
3 tablespoons coarsely chopped unsalted peanuts
12 candied cherries

Soak the raisins in 2 tablespoons of the rum for 1 hour. Peel the bananas and slice them in half lengthwise, then across. Sprinkle them with the lemon juice to keep them from discoloring. Cream the butter with the confectioners' sugar until it is pale and smooth. Beat in the remaining 2 tablespoons rum.

Scoop out a cavity about 1/4 inch deep the length of each banana piece and stuff with the rum butter cream. Sprinkle with the chopped peanuts and rum-soaked raisins. Decorate with the candied cherries. Chill for 2 to 3 hours before serving.

Yield: 6 servings.

# Fruit Jelly

$\mathcal{B}$iting into any fruit "jelly" in the Caribbean, you'll notice the resemblance to an American commercial product with a quite similar name. But you'll also notice that the marriage of unflavored gelatin and fresh juice from nearly any tropical fruit produces a flavor apart from anything that comes in a box. Island cooks point out, by the way, that fresh pineapple juice must be boiled before use in a jelly because something in its chemistry prevents the dessert from setting.

1/2 cup water
3 envelopes (1/4 oz each) unflavored gelatin
5 cups tropical fruit juice, such as tangerine, soursop, tamarind, or guava
1/2 to 1 cup sugar, to taste
Chunks of tropical fruit (optional)
Whipped cream (optional)

In a large saucepan over medium heat, warm the water and sprinkle in the gelatin, stirring until completely dissolved. Remove the pan from the heat and stir in the fruit juice. Taste for sweetness and add as much sugar as desired, stirring until the sugar has dissolved.

If you wish to add fruit to the jelly, pour three-quarters of the mixture into a mold and refrigerate until set. Then set the fruit atop the set jelly and pour the remaining juice into the mold. Chill until set. Serve with whipped cream, if desired.

Yield: 8 servings.

# Skewered Gooseberries

$\mathcal{T}$his unusual presentation of these round, tart, greenish yellow berries hails from the French West Indies. If you can't find fresh gooseberries, try your favorite berry or substitute chunks or sections of your favorite tropical fruit. As far as I'm concerned, it's the idea of skewering the fruit that makes this dessert.

4 cups fresh gooseberries
2 cups water
2 cups sugar
2 sticks cinnamon

The night before this dish will be served, prepare the gooseberries by removing the stems and blossoms and pricking the skin with a fork. Place in enough water to cover, seal the bowl with plastic wrap, and let stand overnight.

In a large saucepan combine the 2 cups water with the sugar and bring to a slow boil over medium heat. Stir until the sugar dissolves and a thick syrup forms. Drain the berries and add to the syrup along with the cinnamon sticks. Simmer for 15 to 20 minutes. With a slotted spoon remove the berries from the syrup and let cool. Thread the berries onto twenty 12-inch-long wooden skewers and serve.

Yield: about 20 skewers.

# Tamarind Bananas

My Jamaican friend Helen Willinsky, who sells a line of Caribbean food products from just outside Atlanta, came up with the wonderful idea of covering bananas with a sauce of tamarind and apricot before baking them. In her book *Jerk: Barbecue from Jamaica*, she also suggests that with the addition of a little Dijon mustard to the sauce it becomes a terrific partner to medallions of pork.

1 can (8 oz) sweetened tamarind nectar
4 ounces apricot jam
2 tablespoons honey
4 ripe bananas
1/4 cup flaked sweetened coconut
1/4 cup slivered almonds
1 tablespoon brown sugar
2 tablespoons unsalted butter, melted
Juice of 1 lime or lemon

Prepare the sauce by combining the tamarind nectar and the apricot jam in a saucepan over medium-high heat. Bring to a boil, and continue to boil until the mixture thickens, then stir in the honey. (This recipe yields about 1 1/2 cups sauce, so you'll have some left for other uses.)

Preheat the oven to 350 degrees F. Peel the bananas and split lengthwise. Arrange them in a buttered shallow casserole and spoon 1/4 cup sauce over the top. Sprinkle with the coconut and almonds. Mix the brown sugar with the melted butter and pour over the bananas. Bake for 20 minutes. If the bananas are not quite ripe, add 10 more minutes of baking. Serve hot.

Yield: 4 servings.

# Mangoes and Cream

Once in a while in the Caribbean, it seems the simpler the better. This dessert is as simple and sweet as peaches and cream, yet it packs the special punch of the islands.

2 large fresh mangoes, peeled and sliced
1 cup whipping cream
1 cup plain yogurt
Brown sugar, for sprinkling

Arrange the mango slices on 6 individual serving dishes. Beat the cream in a bowl until it is thick. Add the yogurt, beating again until the mixture is free of lumps. Pour over the mangoes. Sprinkle liberally with brown sugar and refrigerate for 4 to 5 hours before serving.
Yield: 6 servings.

*According to author John McPhee, in his delightful book* Oranges, *the fruit's pilgrimage from its origins near the South China Sea "closely and sometimes exactly kept pace with the major journeys of civilization." Oranges traveled down into the Malay Archipelago, across the ocean to Africa, across the African deserts into the Mediterranean, thence to the Americas. It was Arab traders who transported oranges to Africa, Islamic warriors to conquered Spain, and Spanish conquistadors to the New World. Oranges were growing all across the Caribbean by the beginning of the sixteenth century.*

# Piña con Ron

$\mathcal{H}$ ere's a dessert that even simpler than Mangoes and Cream—and equally popular in the Caribbean. This name and this recipe hail from Puerto Rico, yet the notion turns up on Martinique and elsewhere. From island to island, the main variation is the darkness of the rum preferred. In your own kitchen, of course, the choice is yours.

2 small ripe pineapples
Rum, to taste

Prepare the pineapples by slicing them lengthwise into thirds. Keep the leaves on—merely cut through them. Carefully carve the flesh from each piece of pineapple shell in a single piece. Cut off the core. Slice the flesh in half lengthwise and then crosswise, making bite-sized pieces. Return the pieces to the pineapple shell. Pour on rum to taste, and serve.
Yield: 6 servings.

*The notion of a rainbow-hued fruit stand is not new to visitors from the north, even if the variety and freshness of the produce might be. Far more exotic are the street vendors—known as "higglers" in the English-speaking islands—who carry the fruit in baskets balanced on their heads. With every step, they chant their wares, part open-air opera and part prayerful litany. "Cherimoya, carambola, mamey, sapote . . ."*

# Pies & Tarts

What a rich and sweet terrain this Caribbean cuisine is, offering us myriad ways of making a lush filling and pouring it into a flaky pie crust. In this collection there is the traditional breakdown into pies that are baked in their crust and those in a crust already baked. Beyond that, tradition just might take you in some directions you're not expecting to go.

I have included my favorite version of the lime pie so associated with the Florida Keys, along with favorites or soon-to-be favorites built around pineapple and coconut. Yet you can't really fault me for bias when the recipes also include passion fruit, sweet potato, cho-cho (also called chayote, christophine, or vegetable pear), guava, plantain, currant, and prune—not to mention a chocolate rum pie so exquisite it's been the talk of Kingston, Jamaica, for decades.

I have two special favorites among the pies, both as much for their stories as anything else. For me, sweet potato pie is a striking reminder of the African heritage that pulls so many cultures not usually found together into a focus we recognize as Caribbean. And the tale of the lowly cho-cho—how it found fame in a pie as the island's own version of all-American apple pie—speaks eloquently of the pride the Caribbean people are finally discovering and indeed have deserved from their beginnings.

# Passion Fruit Pie

Though I discovered this pie in Barbados, the chef who prepared it for me cited his own inspiration as a "little old lady in St. Thomas." So things go in the Caribbean!

1 cup ground vanilla wafers
1/3 cup unsalted butter, at room temperature
1/4 cup packed brown sugar
14 passion fruits
4 eggs, separated, at room temperature
1/2 cup granulated sugar
1 envelope (1/4 oz) unflavored gelatin
1/2 teaspoon salt
1/8 teaspoon cream of tartar
1/2 cup confectioners' sugar
1/2 cup whipping cream, chilled
1/4 cup finely chopped candied
green citron (optional garnish)

Preheat the oven to 350 degrees F. To prepare the crust, in a medium bowl combine the ground wafers, butter, and brown sugar. Press the mixture into the bottom and up the sides of a 9-inch pie pan. Bake until set, about 8 minutes. Let cool.

Prepare the filling by cutting each passion fruit in half and scooping out the pulp. In a food processor or blender, blend until the pulp separates from the seeds; do not crush the seeds. Strain the puree, then transfer 3/4 cup of it to a heavy medium saucepan. Mix in the egg yolks, followed by the granulated sugar, gelatin, and salt. Cook over low heat, stirring, until the sugar and gelatin are dissolved and the mixture has thickened. Allow to cool, then pour into the baked cookie crust.

In a bowl, beat the egg whites until stiff peaks form, then beat in the cream of tartar and confectioners sugar. In a separate bowl, beat the cream then fold it into the meringue. Spread the meringue over the pie filling and garnish with candied green citron. Chill thoroughly.

Yield: 8 servings.

*In his journal Columbus recorded that the island natives he spotted were "very strong and live largely on a tree melon called 'the fruit of the angels.'" The description is an apt one for the fruit that kept the locals fortified, a fruit known to us as the papaya. It's not really a tree but the stalk of a giant plant that grows 15 to 20 feet tall, with its top an explosion of leaves carrying the heavy dark green fruits. The name papaya was taken by the Spanish from the Carib Indian language, yet this hasn't stopped others from deriving different names. Papaya is known in the Spanish islands as either lechosa or fruta bomba,, the latter a reference to its resemblance to a hand grenade. In the English islands it most often known as the almost-familial pawpaw.*

# Groundnut Molasses Pie

*P*eanuts are still referred to quite colorfully as groundnuts in many parts of the Caribbean. Yet linguistic interest alone doesn't explain the popularity of this pie, which combines chopped peanuts and molasses.

1 recipe Pie Crust (see page 96), unbaked
1/2 cup molasses
1 teaspoon unsalted butter
2 eggs
1/2 cup sugar
1 tablespoon flour
1/2 cup milk
1/4 teaspoon salt
3/4 cup chopped unsalted peanuts
1/2 teaspoon vanilla extract

Preheat the oven to 400 degrees F. Thoroughly prick the base of the unbaked pie crust and bake for 10 minutes. Let cool.

In a medium saucepan over medium-high heat, bring the molasses and butter to a boil, then set the pan aside.

Increase the oven temperature to 425 degrees F. In a medium bowl beat the eggs, then gradually beat in the sugar and flour. Stir in the milk and salt, followed by the cooled molasses mixture. Add the peanuts and vanilla. Pour the filling into the pie crust and bake for 10 minutes. Then reduce the temperature to 325 degrees F and bake until the filling has set, 25 to 30 minutes more. Let cool before serving.

Yield: 6 to 8 servings.

# Lime Pie

This classic turns up most often as Key lime pie—a name that refers to the Florida Keys and imparts a certain flair. Yet pies made with limes remain a staple across the Caribbean, which is just fine with me.

1 cup plus 3 tablespoons sugar
2 tablespoons flour
3 tablespoons cornstarch
1/4 teapoon salt
2 cups boiling water
3 eggs, separated
3/4 cup freshly squeezed lime juice
1 teaspoon grated lime zest
1 tablespoon unsalted butter
1 recipe Pie Crust (see page 96), baked

In a double boiler over hot water, blend the 1 cup sugar, flour, cornstarch, and salt. Stir in the boiling water and cook, stirring, until the mixture thickens. Continue cooking over low heat for 10 minutes, then remove from the heat.

Beat the egg yolks; stir in a small amount of the hot mixture, then whisk back into the hot mixture and cook, stirring, 2 minutes. Add the lime juice, zest, and butter. Pour the filling into the baked crust.

Preheat the oven to 350 degrees F. To prepare the meringue, beat the egg whites in a medium bowl until stiff but not dry, adding the 3 tablespoons sugar a little at a time. Spoon the meringue over the top of the pie and bake just until the top starts to brown. Refrigerate until chilled, then serve.

Yield: 8 servings.

# Chocolate Rum Pie

This is that rarity in the Caribbean, a recipe that uses chocolate. Nonetheless, it began turning up on dessert tables around Kingston, Jamaica, some 20 years ago, the creation of a candlemaker named Amy O'Brien. I'll keep my candle burning for this Chocolate Rum Pie anytime.

1 cup ground vanilla wafers
1/3 cup unsalted butter, at room temperature
1/4 cup packed brown sugar
1/2 cup granulated sugar
1 envelope (1/4 oz) unflavored gelatin
1/8 teaspoon salt
2 eggs, separated
1 cup milk
1 package (6 oz) semisweet chocolate pieces (1 cup)
1/2 cup dark rum
1 cup whipping cream
1 teaspoon vanilla extract
Whipped cream, for topping
Pecan halves, for garnish

Preheat the oven to 350 degrees F. To prepare the crust, in a medium bowl combine the ground wafers, butter, and brown sugar. Press the mixture into the bottom and up the sides of a 9-inch pie pan. Bake until set, about 8 minutes. Let cool.

In a heavy saucepan combine the granulated sugar, gelatin, and salt. Beat the egg yolks, then stir them in along with the milk. Cook, stirring, over low heat until slightly thickened. Remove from the heat. Add the chocolate pieces and stir until melted, then add the rum. Chill in the refrigerator until partially set.

Beat the egg whites until soft peaks form. Fold them into the chocolate mixture. Whip the 1 cup cream with the vanilla, then layer this with the chocolate mixture into the cooled pie crust, ending with whipped cream. Swirl the top to create a marbled effect. Chill until the filling is firm. Decorate with the whipped cream and the pecan halves. Serve well chilled.

Yield: 8 servings.

# St. Kitts Coconut Pie

Coconut milk joins forces with evaporated milk in this simple celebration of one of the Caribbean's most beloved flavors.

2 large eggs
1/4 cup sugar
1/2 cup grated unsweetened coconut
1/2 cup evaporated milk
1/2 cup Coconut Milk (see page 120)
1 tablespoon unsalted butter
1 recipe Pie Crust (see page 96), unbaked

Preheat the oven to 450 degrees F. In a medium bowl beat the eggs with the sugar until light and fluffy, then incorporate the grated coconut, evaporated milk, Coconut Milk, and butter. Pour into the pie crust and bake for 10 minutes. Reduce the heat to 350 degrees F and bake until the custard is set and the crust is lightly browned, 25 to 30 minutes longer. Let cool before serving.

Yield: 6 servings.

*As Christopher Columbus sailed past Trinidad on his third New World voyage, he recorded his emotion at the sight of shores "so fair and so verdant and so full of trees and palms. . . . Every tree is pleasant to the sight and good for food."*

# Sweet Potato Pie

$\mathcal{I}$'ve always loved Caribbean desserts created around sweet potatoes. Particularly in straightforward renderings such as this pie, they speak in poignant terms of the West African coast that many islanders remember in their foods when all other memories have faded.

Among the types of sweet potatoes available are the incorrectly named Louisiana yam (not a true yam at all), and the less-sweet boniato favored in the islands.

1 tablespoon unsalted butter, softened
2 cups mashed cooked sweet potatoes
2 eggs, beaten
1 cup evaporated milk
3/4 cup packed light brown sugar
1/2 cup light corn syrup
1 teaspoon vanilla extract
1/2 teaspoon ground ginger
1/2 teaspoon ground cinnamon
1/2 teaspoon freshly grated nutmeg
1 recipe Pie Crust (see page 96), unbaked
Whipped cream, for topping

Preheat the oven to 375 degrees F. In a medium bowl beat the butter, sweet potatoes, and eggs until combined. Mix in the evaporated milk, brown sugar, corn syrup, vanilla, ginger, cinnamon, and nutmeg. Pour the mixture into the pie crust and bake for 35 to 45 minutes. Let cool.

Decorate with whipped cream and serve.

Yield: 8 servings.

# Cream Cheese and Rum Pie

Although related to the dessert we mistakenly call "cheesecake," this pie spiked with dark rum is Caribbean through and through. I particularly like the topping of sour cream flavored with sugar, cinnamon, and rum.

1 cup unsalted butter
18 graham crackers, crushed
3 small packages (3 oz each) cream cheese, softened
1 teaspoon whipping cream, or as needed
1/2 cup plus 5 tablespoons sugar
2 eggs, beaten
1 1/2 teaspoons dark rum
1 pint sour cream
1/8 teaspoon ground cinnamon

Preheat the oven to 370 degrees F. Prepare the crust by melting the butter, then adding the crushed graham crackers. Mix well. Line a 9-inch pie pan with this mixture and bake for 5 minutes. Set aside to cool but leave the oven on.

Prepare the filling by beating together the cream cheese, whipping cream, and the 1/2 cup sugar until smooth, adding a little more cream if necessary. Beat in the eggs and 1 teaspoon of the dark rum. Fill the pie crust and bake for 20 minutes.

Meanwhile, blend the sour cream with the 5 tablespoons sugar, cinnamon, and the remaining 1/2 teaspoon rum. Spread this over the pie and return to the oven for 5 minutes. Chill thoroughly before serving.

Yield: 8 servings.

# Cho-Cho Pie

*I*f desserts were judged by the story they have to tell, I'd give my grand prize to Cho-Cho Pie. You see, there was a time when islanders were ashamed of the fact they didn't have apples to make the pies they tasted from other parts of the world. They used their own humble cho-chos, wishing they could be apples. Now many visitors to the Caribbean, tasting this pie, find themselves wishing their apples could be cho-chos.

4 cho-chos (chayote, vegetable pear, or christophene)
1 cup water
6 whole cloves or allspice berries
1 cup sugar
Juice of 2 limes
2 recipes Pie Crust (see page 96), unbaked
Zest of 1 lime

Preheat the oven to 400 degrees F. Peel and core the cho-chos, then cut the flesh into small pieces. In a medium saucepan simmer them in the water with the cloves until they are tender. Remove the cho-chos from the pan and reserve. Discard the spices. Add the sugar and lime juice to the remaining juice. Simmer until thick and syrupy, then allow to cool.

Line a pie pan with half the pastry and arrange the reserved cho-cho pieces on it. Sprinkle with the lime zest and pour the cooled liquid over the top. Roll out the remaining pastry and cover the pie. Seal or crimp the edges, cutting two slits in the top to let the steam escape. Bake until brown, about 45 minutes. Let cool before serving.

Yield: 8 servings.

# Papaya Pie

This terrific-tasting pie actually uses both pie crust and sponge cake in a manner first encountered in Puerto Rico. The recipe may or may not be traditional; but once you've tasted this celebration of fresh papaya, that won't seem to matter much.

4 cups milk
1/2 cup unsalted butter
1 cup sugar
4 egg yolks, beaten
2 whole eggs, beaten
1/2 cup cornstarch
1/8 teaspoon salt
1/2 teaspoon vanilla extract
1 recipe Pie Crust (see page 96), baked
1 recipe Sponge Cake (see page 52),cut in 1/4-inch slices
1 large ripe papaya, sliced
Whipped cream, for topping

In a heavy saucepan combine the milk, butter, sugar, beaten egg yolks, whole beaten eggs, cornstarch, salt, and vanilla. Cook over medium heat until the mixture comes to a boil. Remove from the heat and allow to cool.

Cover the baked pie crust with the Sponge Cake slices, then add a layer of sliced papaya. Pour in one-quarter of the cooled pastry cream, followed by another layer of papaya. Continue until all the fruit and cream are used, ending with the pastry cream. Decorate with whipped cream and serve.

Yield: 8 servings.

# Bajan Pineapple Pie

This beloved pie, which I first tasted in Barbados, is in many ways a tropical rendition of the pastry-covered apple pies served since colonial times in the United States. Once again, despite differences of climate and present culture, the similarities to our New World colonial past are evident.

2 recipes Pie Crust (see page 96), unbaked
1 large pineapple, peeled, cored, and chopped (about 3 cups)
1 cup sugar
1/4 cup flour
1/4 teaspoon freshly grated nutmeg
1/8 teaspoon ground cinnamon
1/8 teaspoon salt
3 tablespoons unsalted butter
Water, if needed

Preheat the oven to 400 degrees F. Thoroughly prick the base of the pie crust and bake for 10 minutes. Let cool.

In a medium saucepan combine the pineapple, sugar, flour, nutmeg, cinnamon, and salt. Cook, stirring, over low heat until the mixture thickens. Remove from the heat and stir in the butter and a little water, if needed; the mixture should be creamy and pourable. Let cool.

Increase the oven temperature to 425 degrees F. Pour the filling into the partially baked pie crust and cover with the remaining rolled-out pastry. Seal the edges with a bit of water, crimping with a fork. Make three slits in the top to allow steam to escape. Bake for 10 minutes, then reduce the temperature to 325 degrees F and bake until the crust is lightly browned, about 30 minutes more. Let cool before serving.

Yield: 6 to 8 servings.

# Coconut Cream Pie

This recipe from Jamaica is quite different from St. Kitts Coconut Pie, being cooked stovetop, then poured into a baked pie shell rather than being baked in the shell. Not surprisingly, considering its ingredients and its name, it's a good deal creamier as well. Both are scrumptious.

1 cup sugar
1/2 cup cornstarch
1/2 teaspoon salt
3 cups hot milk
3 egg yolks, beaten
1/2 teaspoon almond extract
1 teaspoon vanilla extract
2 cups grated unsweetened coconut
1 recipe Pie Crust (see page 96), baked
1 cup whipping cream

In a medium saucepan combine the sugar, cornstarch, and salt. Gradually add the milk, stirring until smooth. Bring to a boil over medium heat and boil for 2 minutes. Remove from the heat.

Stir some of this hot mixture into the egg yolks, then pour back into the mixture in the saucepan, stirring constantly.

Cook over low heat until the mixture is bubbly and thick, about 5 minutes. Pour the filling into a medium bowl. Stir in the extracts and half the coconut. Chill for 1 hour in the refrigerator, then pour into the baked pie crust. Whip the cream and spread over the pie. Top with the remaining coconut and serve.

Yield: 8 servings.

# Plantain Tarts

*I*t's part of the English legacy in the Caribbean: eating tarts right out of a host of nursery rhymes. This particular recipe spices up what otherwise would be typical pastry crust, then fills it with equally flavorful mashed plantains.

## Pastry
2 cups flour
1 cup vegetable shortening
1 teaspoon ground cinnamon
1/4 teaspoon freshly grated nutmeg
1/4 teaspoon salt
About 2 tablespoons ice water

## Filling
1 cup mashed very ripe plantain
1/2 cup sugar
1 tablespoon unsalted butter
1/2 teaspoon freshly grated nutmeg
1 teaspoon vanilla extract
1 tablespoon raisins

To prepare the pastry, combine half the flour with the shortening in a medium bowl. Blend with a pastry cutter until the mixture forms pea-sized crumbs. Add the remaining flour, cinnamon, nutmeg, and salt, then cut again until the mixture resembles bread crumbs. Add enough ice water to hold the mixture together, then form in a ball. Cover with plastic wrap and chill in refrigerator 1 to 2 hours.

To prepare the filling, in a medium saucepan combine the plantain, sugar, and butter. Warm throughly over low heat. Remove from the heat and stir in the nutmeg, vanilla, and raisins. Let cool.

Preheat the oven to 450 degrees F. Turn the dough out on a lightly floured board and roll 1/8 inch thick. Cut the dough into six 4-inch circles and spoon some filling into the center of each. Fold the dough over the filling and seal by crimping the edges with a fork.

Place the tarts on an ungreased baking sheet. Prick the top of each with a fork and bake until the pastry is delicately brown, about 30 minutes. Let cool before serving.

Yield: 6 servings.

*If you order a "wedding cake" in Jamaica, Barbados, or Antigua, don't hold your breath for some towering white confection with a plastic bride and groom on top. A wedding cake here is a dark fruitcake made with candied lime, orange, and citron, and invariably steeped heavily in rum. It is also known as bride's cake, Christmas cake, or, most commonly, black cake. An English cookbook written in 1813 provides a recipe for wedding cake most notable for its stern instructions: "Beat in your sugar a quarter of an hour" and the egg yolks "half an hour at least." Today in the Caribbean, the same directions are likely to be given.*

# Guava Pie

*H*ere's a very traditional island pie. In fact, it's usually a safe bet that any recipe that's this simple is traditional. The sweet flavor of guava—so beloved across the Caribbean as jelly and jam—makes this pastry-covered pie well worth slicing into.

12 fresh guavas
2 cups water
1 cup sugar
2 recipes Pie Crust (see page 96), unbaked

Preheat the oven to 400 degrees F. Peel the guavas, then cut them in half and remove the seeds. In a medium pan cook the guavas with the water and sugar for 10 minutes, then remove and reserve the fruit.

Reduce the remaining liquid over high heat until it thickens. Line a 9-inch pie pan with half the pastry and fill it with the reserved guavas. Pour the thickened syrup over the top. Cover the filling with the remaining pastry and make 2 slits to allow steam to escape. Bake until brown, about 45 minutes. Serve warm.

Yield: 8 servings.

# Prune Tart

This tart hails from the Dominican Republic, the Spanish-speaking half of the large island shared with French-speaking Haiti. Around the capital of Santo Domingo, this prune tart is known as tarta de ciruelas pasas.

1 pound dried pitted prunes
1/4 cup flour
1 cup sugar
1/4 teaspoon salt
1/2 teaspoon ground cinnamon
1 cup whipping cream
1 recipe Pie Crust (see page 96), unbaked
Whipped cream, for topping

Preheat the oven to 400 degrees F. Set aside 18 of the prunes and finely chop the rest. In a medium bowl sift together the flour, sugar, salt, and cinnamon, then stir in the 1 cup cream. Add the chopped prunes and incorporate thoroughly. Pour the filling into the unbaked pie crust and make a circle with the whole prunes around the rim.

Bake until the filling is set, 35 to 40 minutes. Serve with whipped cream.
Yield: 6 servings.

# Currant Tartlets

The English Caribbean in particular has always conducted a "currant affair"—a passion that here is turned here into a carmelized topping for a lush cooked custard. This recipe can be changed a bit to make one large tart. But I prefer it divided into six individual small pastry shells.

## Pastry
2 cups flour
1 cup vegetable shortening
1 teaspoon ground cinnamon
1/4 teaspoon freshly grated nutmeg
1/4 teaspoon salt
About 2 tablespoons ice water

## Filling
1/4 cup fresh currants
or 1/4 cup dried currants soaked in warm water
for 30 minutes, then drained
1/2 cup Cointreau or other orange-flavored liqueur
2 cups milk
1/2 teaspoon vanilla extract
3 egg yolks
1 cup sugar
1/4 cup flour
1/4 cup water

To prepare the pastry, combine half the flour with the shortening in a medium bowl. Blend with a pastry cutter until the mixture forms pea-sized crumbs. Add the remaining flour, cinnamon, nutmeg, and salt, then cut again until the mixture resembles bread crumbs. Add enough ice water to hold the mixture together, then form in a ball. Cover with plastic wrap and chill in refrigerator 1 to 2 hours.

Meanwhile, prepare the filling. Combine the currants with half the liqueur in a small saucepan. Let stand while preparing the custard. In a medium saucepan bring the milk and vanilla just to the boiling point. In a small bowl beat the egg yolks and 3/4 cup of the sugar until light and fluffy. Beat in the flour. Gradually beat in a small amount of the hot milk mixture. Pour the egg mixture into the remaining milk and cook over medium heat, stirring constantly, until the mixture thickens. Cook for 5 minutes more, continuing to stir. Let the custard cool, then stir in the remaining liqueur. Set aside.

Preheat the oven to 450 degrees F. Turn the pastry dough out on a lightly floured board and roll 1/8 inch thick. Cut the dough into six 4-inch circles and press into small individual tart pans. Prick the bottom of each with a fork and bake until the pastry is delicately brown, about 10 to 12 minutes. Let cool, then divide the custard evenly among the tart shells.

In a small saucepan combine the water and the remaining 1/4 cup sugar. Cook over medium heat until the mixture just begins to carmelize and turn golden brown. Bring the reserved liqueur-soaked currants to a boil and simmer for 5 minutes. Blend in the carmelized sugar. Top the custard tarts with the carmelized currants and serve.

Yield: 6 servings.

# Jamaican Orange Tart

*I* love the way mainstream oranges are still referred to as "Seville oranges" in Jamaica, reminding us that they were brought into the region by the Spaniards along with so many other tropical fruits. If the islands today seem a Garden of Eden, it was long a garden tended by Spaniards to feed their far-flung empire.

### Tarts
1/4 cup unsalted butter
1 tablespoon grated orange zest
1/4 cup orange juice
1/4 cup light rum
1/8 teaspoon salt
3/4 cup sugar
2 egg yolks
3 eggs
1/2 cup whipping cream
1 recipe Pie Crust (see page 96), baked

### Glazed Orange Slices
1/4 cup water
1 cup sugar
1 orange, thinly sliced

In the top of a double boiler over simmering water, melt the butter and add the orange zest, juice, rum, salt, and sugar. In a small bowl beat together the egg yolks and whole eggs, then add to the orange mixture. Stirring constantly, cook over the simmering water until the mixture is thick and shiny. Spoon into a bowl and let cool.

In a chilled small bowl, whip the cream until it is very thick, then fold it into the egg-orange mixture. Pour the filling into the pie crust.

To glaze the orange slices, in a small saucepan bring the water and sugar to a boil, then reduce the heat and simmer 2 to 3 minutes. Dip the orange slices in the syrup for 1 minute. Let cool on plastic wrap. Garnish the tart with the glazed orange slices. Chill before serving.

Yield: 8 servings.

# Pie Crust

All but a handful of pies and tarts in this chapter use a basic pastry shell, baked or unbaked, and a few require a double quantity for a traditional covered pie. Here is a recipe for a single quantity that will work.

1/3 cup plus 1 tablespoon vegetable shortening
1 cup flour, plus more for dusting
1/2 teaspoon salt
2 to 3 tablespoons cold water

In a medium bowl, using your fingers or a pastry cutter, combine the shortening, the 1 cup flour, and salt until the mixture resembles coarse crumbs. Pour in just enough water to form a dough. Gather the dough into a ball, dust with flour, and cover with plastic wrap. Refrigerate for 30 minutes.

On a floured work surface, roll out the ball to an 11-inch circle. Place in a 9-inch pie pan and crimp the edge.

To use as a prebaked crust, preheat the oven to 425 degrees F and bake until golden brown, about 15 minutes. Be sure to use one of the two popular "blind baking" techniques for a fine baked crust, filling the crust with a pound of either dried beans or the metal weights sold in specialty shops.

Yield: one 9-inch crust.

# Puddings & Pones

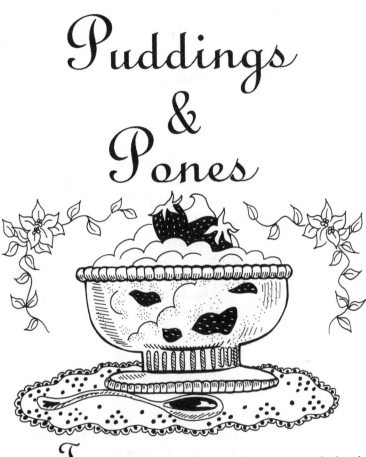

The sheer variety and offhand creativity of island puddings and their next-of-kin pones are outdone only by their absolute quirkiness. There are, however, a few clarifying comments to be offered up front.

Those puddings that are boiled or baked in one pot tend to be the most ancient cultural legacies of Africa or the Indian Americas. Those puddings that require precise measurement to achieve a certain texture or density, or that require tricky European techniques, or that, quite simply, require refrigeration tend to be newer twists added by the immigrant group with the most invested in those particular dishes.

That said, the map of Caribbean puddings and pones is vast, and it's still crying out for exploration. From desserts created from leftovers such as bread and rice to sophisticated French-kissed custards, from cornmeal pones that could almost be side dishes to Puerto Rican Tembleque (the perfect spin on Spanish flan), you're steering through dazzling waters when you're navigating these.

# Rice Pudding with Guava Sauce

The use of rice to make puddings is hardly unique to the Caribbean, yet the touches that enliven this stylish molded version are island all the way. Cuban markets and specialty food stores are the best places to look for sweetened coconut cream and guava marmalade.

## Pudding
2 cups short-grain rice
3 cups water
3 cups half-and-half
2/3 cup sugar
1/8 teaspoon salt
1 large strip lime zest
2 envelopes (1/4 oz each) unflavored gelatin
1 cup cold water
1 can (9 1/2 oz) sweetened coconut cream
1 teaspoon vanilla extract
2 cups whipping cream
Sliced fresh guavas, for garnish

## Guava Sauce
1 can (15 oz) guava marmalade
1 tablespoon dark rum

Let the rice soak in the 3 cups water overnight, then drain, transfer to a large saucepan, and add the half-and-half, sugar, salt, and lime zest. Cook over low heat until the rice is very tender, 20 to 30 minutes.

Meanwhile, soften the gelatin in the 1 cup cold water. Add to the hot cooked rice and stir to dissolve the gelatin. Stir in the coconut cream and vanilla and set aside to cool.

Whip the cream until soft peaks form, then fold it into the cooled rice mixture. Pour into a 4-quart ring mold, cover, and chill overnight to set.

Prepare the sauce by heating the marmalade in a heavy saucepan over medium heat, stirring constantly until the volume is reduced by one-fourth. Stir in the rum and chill.

To serve, unmold the pudding onto a platter, fill the center with the sauce, and garnish with guava slices.

Yield: 10 to 12 servings.

*It is said that the only proper place to eat a ripe mango is in the bathtub—the fruit is that juicy. But there is a technique for removing the flesh from its stone, or pit, which I'll share right here. Lay the mango on its flattest side and cut a thick slice off the top. Turn the fruit over and do the same thing on the other side. These two halves can be served like avocado and devoured with a spoon. The flesh still clinging to the stone must be attacked a bit at a time—cut off in chunks or eaten directly using several napkins.*

# Pitch Lake Pudding

*I*t's hard to imagine that a seepage of natural asphalt could inspire anything this lovely, but that's exactly what Pitch Lake in Trinidad has done. This pudding is popular by this name with both Trinidadians and Bajans. It also turns up here and there as Mousse Antillaise.

12 tablespoons unsalted butter, cut into small pieces
3 tablespoons granulated or powdered instant coffee
3/4 cup boiling water
3 cups unsweetened cocoa powder
6 eggs, separated
2 cups sugar
1/3 cup Curacao or Grand Marnier
1/8 teaspoon salt
1 cup whipping cream, chilled and whipped until stiff

Melt the butter over moderate heat in the top of a double boiler, then set the pan over simmering but not boiling water. Dissolve the instant coffee in the 3/4 cup boiling water and stir into the melted butter. Sift in the cocoa about 1/4 cup at a time, beating constantly with a wire whisk or large spoon. Beat until the mixture is a smooth paste. Keep the cocoa paste warm over low heat.

In a deep bowl beat the egg yolks for about 1 minute with an electric mixer or hand beater. Beat in the sugar 1/4 cup at a time, continuing to beat until the yolks turn pale yellow and are thick enough to fall in a ribbon when the beater is removed. Beat in the cocoa paste 1/2 cup at a time. Beat in the liqueur and set the mixture aside.

In a separate bowl beat the egg whites and salt together with a wire whisk or an electric mixer until stiff peaks form. Stir one-quarter of the whites into the cocoa mixture, then pour this over the remaining egg whites. Fold together gently.

Ladle the pudding into a 1-quart souffle dish or a large serving bowl, or prepare individual servings in dessert dishes. Refrigerate for at least 3 hours. When ready to serve, spread a light layer of whipped cream over the pudding.

Yield: 8 servings.

# Sweet Potato Pudding

The Caribbean's timeless love affair with sweet potatoes links its people forever with their shared past in Africa. Among the types of sweet potatoes available are the incorrectly named Louisiana yam (not a true yam at all), and the less-sweet boniato favored in the islands. In addition to pies, tarts, and a host of other sweet creations made with sweet potatoes, there's this wonderful (and simple) hot pudding from the misty Blue Mountains of Jamaica.

3 pounds sweet potatoes, peeled and grated
1/2 teaspoon freshly grated nutmeg
1-inch piece fresh ginger, grated
1 1/2 cups packed brown sugar
1 teaspoon salt
1 can (14 oz) sweetened condensed milk
1 teaspoon vanilla extract
1 1/2 cups water
1 cup unsalted butter, softened

Preheat the oven to 375 degrees F. Butter a 9-inch square baking dish and set aside. In a large bowl mix the grated sweet potatoes, nutmeg, ginger, brown sugar, and salt. In a medium bowl combine the milk, vanilla, water, and butter, then mix into the sweet potato mixture.

Pour into the prepared dish and bake until the center is set, about 1 1/2 hours. Let cool before serving.

Yield: about 20 servings.

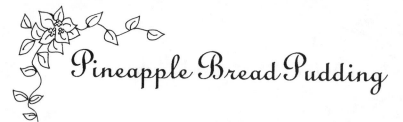

# Pineapple Bread Pudding

As throughout the Old World, hardened settlers of the New World learned to let nothing go to waste. Day-old French bread seemed a tempting excuse for embellishing the traditional bread pudding with the fruits, spices, and rum of the islands. This dish combines the best elements of bread pudding and the popular Caribbean drink, the pina colada.

## Pudding

1 day-old loaf (10 oz) French bread, broken into chunks
2 cups milk
1 can (15 oz) sweetened coconut cream
2 cups sugar
1/2 cup unsalted butter, melted
3 eggs
2 tablespoons vanilla extract
1 can (8 oz) crushed pineapple
1 cup shredded unsweetened coconut
1 cup chopped nuts, such as pecans
1 teaspoon ground cinnamon
1/2 teaspoon freshly grated nutmeg

## Rum Sauce

1/2 cup unsalted butter
1 1/2 cups sugar
1 egg yolk
1/2 cup dark rum

Preheat the oven to 350 degrees F. Butter a 9-inch square baking dish and set aside. Combine all the pudding ingredients in a large bowl and mix until moist but not soupy. Pour into the prepared dish and set on the middle rack of the oven. Bake until the top is golden brown, about 1 1/4 hours.

While the pudding is baking, prepare the sauce by creaming the butter and sugar in a saucepan over medium heat until all the butter is absorbed. Remove from the heat and blend in the egg yolk, stirring constantly. Pour in the rum, continuing to stir. The sauce will thicken as it cools (but don't let it cool completely).

To serve, cut the baked pudding into squares and serve on dessert dishes. Top each square with the warm sauce.

Yield: about 20 servings.

*Lady Janet Schaw, traveling through the West Indies in the mid-1700s, described what she saw as wastefulness in the preparation of pineapple. "When I first came here," she wrote of Antigua, "I could not bear to see so much of the pineapple thrown away. They cut off a deep paring, then cut out the firm part of the heart, which takes away not much less than half the pineapple." Rather quickly, though, the abundance of the islands took its toll. "Only observe how easy it is to become extravagant. I can now feel if the least bit of rind remains; and as to the heart, heavens! Who would eat the nasty heart of a pineapple."*

# Puddin di Coco

With its marriage of lush coconut custard and pleasantly crunchy grated lime rind, this sauced pudding is one of the most enjoyable desserts I tasted on Aruba in the Dutch Caribbean.

## Pudding

2 envelopes (1/4 oz each) unflavored gelatin
1/4 cup dark rum
3 eggs, separated
1/2 cup sugar
1 cup Coconut Milk(see page 120)
1 cup milk
1/8 teaspoon salt
1 cup whipping cream

## Lime Sauce

1/2 cup sugar
1 tablespoon cornstarch
1 cup water
3 tablespoons unsalted butter, softened
1/2 teaspoon grated lime zest
1 1/2 tablespoons freshly squeezed lime juice
1/8 teaspoon salt

Dissolve the gelatin in the rum. Beat the egg yolks until creamy. In a medium saucepan combine the beaten yolks and 1/4 cup of the sugar, then stir in the Coconut Milk and the milk. Cook the mixture over low heat, stirring constantly, until it thickens. Blend in the gelatin mixture and chill in the refrigerator.

Beat the egg whites with the salt until they are stiff but not dry, then gradually beat in the remaining 1/4 cup sugar. In a separate bowl beat the cream until it is stiff. Beat the chilled custard mixture with a wire whisk, then fold it gently into the egg white mixture. Fold in the whipped cream. Mound the pudding in a serving bowl and chill well.

To prepare the sauce, in a small saucepan combine the sugar and cornstarch with the water. Cook over low heat, stirring constantly, until it thickens. Remove the pan from the heat and stir in the butter, lime zest, lime juice, and salt. Chill well. Just before serving, beat the sauce with a wire whisk.

Serve the pudding in the bowl with the sauce on the side.

Yield: 6 servings.

*Don't be put off by the name of the ugli fruit, for all who mention it in the Caribbean do so with great affection. A cross between a grapefruit and an orange, the ugli fruit picked up its moniker from Jamaicans who thought it resembled a lumpy, misshapen version of its parents. Yet the ugli's "inner beauty"—its delicate and pleasantly tart flavor—is universally praised.*

# Tembleque

$\mathcal{A}$lthough some Americans encounter "flan" during travels in Spain, many more are making its acquaintance these days during travels to Caribbean islands settled by Spaniards. Simple custards such as this are popular in Cuba and, under the name Tembleque, in Puerto Rico.

4 cups milk
1/8 teaspoon salt
1 cup sugar
8 eggs
1 teaspoon vanilla extract
6 tablespoons unsalted butter

Preheat the oven to 300 degrees F. In a large saucepan combine the milk and salt and heat until bubbles form around the edge of the milk. Remove from the heat and add the sugar, stirring until it is dissolved. Set the mixture aside.

In a large bowl beat the eggs until they are foamy, then gradually stir in the milk-sugar mixture. Add the vanilla and stir well. Melt the butter in a small skillet until it is golden, then use this to coat a 1 1/2-quart tube pan. Pour the custard mixture into the pan. Place the pan in a shallow baking or roasting pan with water about halfway up the sides.

Bake until a knife inserted in the center comes out clean, about 1 hour. Let the custard cool thoroughly before inverting onto a serving platter.

Yield: 6 servings.

# Forgotten Pudding

*I* sometimes think that Caribbean cooks have as much fun naming dishes as they have cooking them or even eating them. As memorable as the Jamaican savories known as Stamp and Go and Rundown, this Dutch island dessert is named after its incredibly easy cooking method. It is placed in the oven, and promptly forgotten.

## Pudding
1/2 cup plus 6 tablespoons sugar
8 egg whites
1/8 teaspoon cream of tartar

## Sauce
3 tablespoons sugar
2 tablespoons flour
1/8 teaspoon salt
3 egg yolks, beaten
1 1/2 cups milk, scalded
1 teaspoon vanilla extract

Preheat the oven to 450 degrees F. Place the 1/2 cup sugar in a small saucepan over medium-high heat and stir until it melts and begins to turn light brown. Pour it immediately into a 1 1/2-quart mold and twirl to coat. Beat the egg whites with the cream of tartar until completely dry, then beat in the 6 tablespoons sugar. Spoon this mixture into the sugar-coated mold. Set the mold in a shallow pan with water halfway up the sides and place in the oven. Turn off the oven and leave the dessert in it for 2 hours.

Prepare the sauce by combining the sugar, flour, and salt in the top of a double boiler over simmering, not boiling, water. Stir in the egg yolks, followed by the scalded milk. Cook over the simmering water, stirring constantly, until the mixture thickens. Let cool, stirring occasionally. Strain out any lumps, if necessary. Then stir in the vanilla.

When ready to serve, unmold the meringue onto a serving platter and spoon the sauce over the top or serve it in a separate bowl.

Yield: 10 servings.

# Crema di Sorsaka

his might strike you as a variant on Bavarian cream; but believe me, with the addition of ripe soursop from the tropics, it's Caribbean through and through. This is a recipe I picked up on Curacao.

2 medium-sized ripe soursops
2 envelopes (1/4 oz each) unflavored gelatin
1/4 cup cold water
1 3/4 cups milk or half-and-half
1/2 cup sugar
1/8 teaspoon salt
1 cup whipping cream
Additional whipped cream, for topping

Peel and seed the soursops, then puree the pulp using a fine sieve, blender, or food processor. Divide the mashed fruit into two equal portions and set aside.

Dissolve the gelatin in the water. In a medium saucepan scald the milk, then stir in 1/4 cup of the sugar and half the salt until dissolved. Blend in the dissolved gelatin, followed by one portion of the soursop puree. Add the remaining 1/4 cup sugar and the rest of the salt to the remaining soursop and chill in the refrigerator. Chill the gelatin mixture until it begins to thicken, then whip until fluffy with a wire whisk.

Beat the 1 cup cream until it is stiff, then fold it into the gelatin mixture. Heap the pudding into a serving dish and chill thoroughly. Just before serving, spoon the sweetened soupsop over the pudding and serve with the additional whipped cream.

Yield: 6 servings.

# Cassava Pone

Despite the convenience of modern kitchen appliances, many island chefs look back with nostalgia to the days when puddings and pones were baked in cast iron over live coals. Sure, they remind the islanders of the drawbacks, as described in the island song: "De bottom bun an' de middle raw." But they keep right on feeling misty-eyed. You can recreate the culinary side of their nostalgia by making this wonderful pone from Jamaica.

1 sweet cassava (about 2 pounds), peeled and grated
1 cup grated unsweetened coconut
1 teaspoon vanilla extract
1/2 teaspoon freshly grated nutmeg
Sugar, to taste
2 cups milk
1 cup Coconut Milk (see page 120)

Preheat the oven to 350 degrees F. Butter a 13- by 9- by 2-inch baking dish and set aside. Combine the grated cassava and coconut in a large bowl. Mix in the vanilla and nutmeg, then sweeten with sugar to taste. Gradually add the milk and Coconut Milk until batter is soft but thick. Add a bit of water if necessary.

Pour the mixture into the prepared baking dish and bake until set, about 1 hour. Serve warm.

Yield: 10 to 12 servings.

# Cho-Cho Pudding

Cho-cho (also called chayote or vegetable pear) pudding is steamed much the same way as Christmas pudding on British islands in the Caribbean. This pudding grows out of the need to devise desserts around the spartan ingredients at hand. Yet it tastes anything but spartan.

4 cloves or allspice berries
1 stick cinnamon
3 large cho-chos
1 1/2 cups unseasoned dry bread crumbs
1/2 cup raisins
1 cup sugar
Juice of 1 lime
2 eggs, well beaten

Butter a 2-quart baking dish and set aside. Bring a medium pot of water to a boil with the cloves and cinnamon, then add the cho-chos and boil until tender. Remove and discard the spices. Mash the cho-chos and wrap the pulp in a clean muslin cloth. Wring out all excess moisture.

Transfer the pulp to a medium bowl and add the bread crumbs, raisins, sugar, and lime juice. Mix well, then stir in the beaten eggs.

Pour the mixture into the prepared baking dish, cover with waxed paper, and secure with a string. Steam the pudding on a rack over boiling water until it shrinks from the sides of the dish, 6 to 8 hours. Remove the damp cover and let the pudding cool in the dish on a wire rack. When cooled, set out on dry paper. The pudding can be served at room temperature, or, to serve warm, wrap it in aluminum foil and heat in a 200 degree F oven.

Yield: 10 servings.

# Flan de Queso

Here is a baked cheese custard that's extremely popular in Puerto Rico, particularly when topped with fresh fruit. It is similar enough to the standard (if always welcome) flan or Tembleque of Spanish origin, yet the cream cheese makes it lighter and even more flavorful.

1 cup sugar, plus more to taste
2 large packages (8 oz each) cream cheese, at room temperature
6 eggs
1 can (14 oz) sweetened condensed milk
1 cup milk
Salt, to taste
1 teaspoon vanilla extract

Preheat the oven to 350 degrees F. Pour the 1 cup sugar into a saucepan and caramelize it over medium heat, stirring with a wooden spoon until it dissolves and begins to turn golden brown. Then use this caramel to coat the bottom and sides of a 1 1/2-quart tube pan. Using a blender or food processor, whip the cream cheese, then blend in the eggs followed by the condensed milk.

Add the milk and salt to taste. Sweeten to taste with additional sugar. Add the vanilla and mix well. Pour the mixture into the coated mold and place this in a larger pan. Fill the pan halfway to the top with water and bake for about 1 to 1 1/2 hours.

Let the pudding cool, then refrigerate. Spoon into a deep-sided dish and serve.

Yield: 6 to 8 servings.

# Breadfruit Pudding

My friend Dunstan Harris, who certainly learned to love breadfruit during his years growing up in Jamaica, found this recipe in Barbados while researching his book *Island Cooking*. He notes that the islanders there often pour a tablespoon of native rum over the pudding while it cools, and I certainly have no intention of breaking with that tradition.

1 breadfruit (about 1 pound), peeled, cooked, and mashed
1/2 cup sugar
1/4 cup unsalted butter, melted
1 tablespoon cornstarch
1 teaspoon grated lemon zest
2 cups half-and-half
2 eggs, lightly beaten
1 teaspoon vanilla extract
2 tablespoons dark rum
Sauce of your choice or ice cream, for accompaniment

Preheat the oven to 350 degrees F. Generously butter a 2-quart baking dish and set aside. Combine all the ingredients in a large bowl and beat until smooth. Pour the batter into the prepared dish and bake until a knife inserted in the center comes out clean, about 1 3/4 hours. Serve warm with your favorite cream sauce, rum sauce, or ice cream.

Yield: 6 to 8 servings.

# Pineapple Rice Pudding

$\mathcal{T}$he traditional Spanish dessert known simply as arroz con leche takes a delightful turn through the tropics in this Caribbean rethinking. Islanders love learning basic recipes from the Old World, then tipping them on their ear with the sweet New World bounty they see all around them.

2 cups cooked white rice
3 cups milk
1/3 cup plus 2 tablespoons granulated sugar
2 tablespoons unsalted butter
1/2 teaspoon salt
3 eggs, separated
1 can (20 oz) crushed pineapple, juice reserved
1 1/2 teaspoons vanilla extract
1/2 cup flaked unsweetened coconut
1 tablespoon cornstarch
1/4 cup packed brown sugar

In a 2-quart saucepan combine the rice, 2 1/2 cups of the milk, the 1/3 cup granulated sugar, 1 tablespoon of the butter, and salt. Cook over medium heat, stirring occasionally, until thick and creamy, about 20 minutes. Beat the egg yolks with the remaining 1/2 cup milk, then add to the rice mixture and cook 1 minute more. Remove from the heat, then add the pineapple and 1 teaspoon of the vanilla. Set aside to cool.

Preheat the oven to 325 degrees F. Butter a 13- by 9-inch baking dish and set aside. In a large bowl beat the egg whites and the remaining 2 tablespoons granulated sugar until the peaks are stiff but not dry. Fold into the cooled rice mixture and turn into the prepared baking dish. Sprinkle with flaked coconut. Bake for 20 to 25 minutes.

Meanwhile, prepare the sauce. In a 1-quart saucepan, combine the reserved pineapple juice with the cornstarch, stirring to dissolve the cornstarch. Add the remaining 1 tablespoon butter, brown sugar, and an additional pinch of salt. Cook until clear and thickened, stirring frequently. Add the remaining 1/2 teaspoon vanilla. To serve, spoon the sauce over the warm pudding.

Yield: 6 servings.

# Sweet Fungi

Fungi, or "funchi" on some islands, is usually a vegetable casserole concocted from little more than cornmeal, sometimes with a few tender pods of okra tossed in. Yet as with many recipes in the Caribbean, the method has been adapted over the generations to produce a sweet. Some cooks call the new dish sweet fungi. This recipe from St. Thomas in the U.S. Virgin Islands seems the best of all the ones I've picked up over the years.

3 cups water
1 teaspoon salt
1 1/4 cups cornmeal
1 tablespoon vegetable shortening
1 tablespoon sugar
1/2 cup milk
1/8 teaspoon ground cinnamon
1/2 cup raisins

In a large saucepan over high heat, bring the water to a rapid boil. Add the salt and cornmeal and stir briskly to prevent lumps from forming. When well combined stir in the shortening, sugar, milk, cinnamon, and raisins. Cover, remove from the heat, and let stand for about 5 minutes, stirring occasionally. Serve hot in a warmed bowl.

Yield: 6 servings.

# Cornmeal Pone with Coconut Topping

From Jamaica comes this luscious baked and topped variant on traditional fungi—like its antecedent a favorite wherever sweets vendors gather across the islands. Good island cooks are quick to remind us that, since cornmeal swells, it is essential to give it sufficient liquid. Otherwise, it turns dry and brittle.

## Pone

2 3/4 cups cornmeal
1/3 cup flour
6 cups Coconut Milk, (see page 120)
2 2/3 cups packed brown sugar
1/2 teaspoon freshly grated nutmeg
1 tablespoon vanilla extract
1/4 cup rum
1 1/3 cups raisins

## Topping

1 cup Coconut Milk, (see page 120)
1/2 cup packed brown sugar
1/4 cup unsalted butter

Preheat the oven to 300 degrees F. Butter a 9- by 9-inch baking pan or line it with aluminum foil; set aside. In a large bowl mix the cornmeal and flour, then gradually stir in the Coconut Milk until a smooth batter forms. Stir in the brown sugar, nutmeg, vanilla, rum, and raisins. The mixture should be liquid rather than paste.

Pour the mixture into the prepared pan and bake until the pone begins to set, about 30 minutes. Meanwhile, mix together the topping ingredients. Pour over the pone and continue baking until a knife inserted in the center comes out clean, about 30 minutes more. Let cool before serving.

Yield: 6 to 8 servings.

# Carrot Pudding

To find the origins of this Caribbean pudding, you must look to the laborers imported from India and their memories of a dessert called *gajar halva*. The recipe, of course, has traveled as far from the Indian subcontinent as these now well-settled island immigrants.

## Pudding

1 cup raisins
1/2 cup dark rum
1/2 cup unsalted butter
1/2 cup sugar
2 cups finely grated carrots
1 cup flour
1/2 teaspoon salt
2 teaspoons baking powder
1 teaspoon ground allspice
2 eggs, beaten

## Rum Sauce

2 tablespoons cornstarch
1 cup cold water
1/4 cup sugar
1 cup dark rum
1 cup orange juice

Butter a 1-quart souffle or baking dish and set aside. Allow the raisins to soak in the rum for at least 1 hour. Preheat the oven to 350 degrees F. Cream the butter with the sugar, then add the carrots and rum-soaked raisins. Mix well.

In a separate bowl sift the flour with the salt, baking powder, and allspice. Add to the carrot mixture and blend. Gently fold in the eggs, then pour the batter into the prepared dish. Bake until a knife inserted in the center comes out clean, about 40 minutes.

Prepare the sauce by mixing the cornstarch with the water in a small saucepan. Add the sugar and cook, stirring constantly, until the sauce thickens. Remove the pan from the heat and stir in the rum and orange juice. Return to the heat and cook, stirring, about 5 minutes, so that all the alcohol in the rum evaporates.

Serve the pudding and the sauce either hot or chilled.

Yield: 4 to 6 servings.

*If you're served a fruit salad in Barbados, you're likely to encounter falernum as well. It's made, apparently only on this island, from a secret recipe that blends rum, sugar syrup, and lime juice. Falernum, it is said, not only improves the flavor of cut-up fruit but prevents it from discoloring. As for the odd name: A very old story tells of a plantation owner who had his favorite slave toss together a libation for some friends. When one of the guests asked for the recipe, the slave replied, "It's fuh me to know and you got fa lern um."*

# Christmas Pudding

Jamaica and Barbados always spring into my mind around Christmastime. After all, where else can you indulge in English Christmas pudding with none of the moist miseries of English winter? Despite the traditional blueprint, however, you will notice more Caribbean spice in this make-ahead version, along with the substitution of omnipresent rum for rare brandy.

## Pudding

1/2 cup flour
1 teaspoon ground allspice
1 teaspoon ground cinnamon
1 teaspoon freshly grated nutmeg
1/2 cup mixed candied citrus peel
1/2 cup chopped blanched almonds
1 tablespoon molasses
1/2 cup unseasoned dry bread crumbs
1/2 cup unsalted butter, melted
1/2 cup packed brown sugar
1/2 cup grated apple
1 small carrot, grated
1 cup raisins
1/2 cup sultanas
1/2 cup currants
Grated zest and juice of 1 lemon
2 eggs
2 cups dark rum
Additional rum, for flaming

## Hard Sauce

1/2 cup unsalted butter
3/4 cup confectioners' sugar
1/4 cup dark rum

In a large bowl stir all the pudding ingredients together. To be traditional, have each family member provide one stir, each making a wish as he or she does so. Let the mixture stand in a cool place for 24 hours so it can "mature."

Press the pudding mixture into a 2-quart heatproof bowl and cover with waxed paper. Secure the paper with a string. Steam the pudding in its bowl on a rack over boiling water 6 to 8 hours.

Remove the damp cover, let the pudding cool, then set it on dry paper. Wrap and store in a cool place up to 2 months. On Christmas Day, steam the pudding 2 to 3 hours to make sure it is heated through.

Prepare the Hard Sauce by creaming the butter in a small bowl until it is light and fluffy. Gradually beat in the confectioners' sugar and rum. Refrigerate until hard. When ready to serve, arrange the pudding on a platter. Heat a ladle full of rum, then ignite with care using a long-stemmed match. Pour the flaming rum over the top of the pudding. Let the flame burn out, then top each serving of pudding with a dollop of Hard Sauce.

Yield: 16 servings.

# Coconut Milk

You can find canned coconut milk now and again—usually with Thai or Indonesian products that turn up in Asian specialty markets. But for your Caribbean sense of well being (not to mention several recipes in this book), you should know what coconut milk is, how it gets to be that way, and how you can make it if you can't find the canned version.

1 large coconut, without cracks and containing water
2 cups boiling water

Preheat the oven to 400 degrees F. With an ice pick or a sharp skewer, pierce the softest eye of the coconut, then drain the liquid and reserve it for another use. (No, this is not coconut milk, but it does make a refreshing drink, as many folks on tours of plantations in the Caribbean have discovered.)

Bake the coconut for 15 minutes, then break it open with a hammer and carefully remove the flesh from the shell using the point of a strong knife. Peel off the brown membrane with a vegetable peeler and cut the coconut meat into small pieces. In a blender or food processor, grind the coconut in batches. When all the meat is ground, return it to the blender or food processor and, with the motor running, add the water in a steady stream. Blend for 1 minute in a blender or 2 minutes in a food processor.

Allow the mixture to cool for at least 5 minutes, then strain it into a bowl through a fine sieve lined with a double thickness of rinsed and squeezed cheesecloth. Press hard on the coconut solids. Bring the corners of the cheesecloth together and squeeze the remaining milk through the sieve into the bowl. Use immediately or refrigerate for up to 3 days.

The coconut solids can be reserved for another use.

Yield: about 2 cups coconut milk.

# Chilled Delights

$\mathcal{A}$t least some of these desserts could qualify for a category or two before now, perhaps with no more liberties than I've taken elsewhere. Yet the fact remains that desserts notable for being chilled do cry out for special attention, particularly when we realize what a strange thing they truly are in the Caribbean.

Refrigeration is such a recent advance in Caribbean history that many islanders with no gray hair remember the thousand ways their mothers had to work around its absence. Mass tourism has brought many conveniences to the Caribbean. And if trade winds still strike me as the world's finest air conditioning, there's no denying that in the realm of cookery things have gotten better with the introduction of artifically created cold. In addition to its obvious sanitation benefits, refrigeration has flung open the doors to many desserts that a wooden box full of ice couldn't handle.

Ice creams and sorbets would seem the most obvious additions to the island dessert cook's bag of tricks. Yet they are only the beginning of an endless list of parfaits, mousses, souffles, bombes, and whips that take flight when the heat of the day gets the cook dreaming of a chilled dessert.

# Trifle

*I*t's no surprise that the English carried their love of trifle to their colonies in the New World. What catches my eye is how skillfully the Caribbean worked its magic on the traditional English recipe.

5 egg yolks
1/4 cup plus 2 tablespoons sugar
1/8 teaspoon salt
1 cup milk
2 cups whipping cream
3 tablespoons plus 1/2 cup dark rum
1 recipe Sponge Cake (see page 52)
6 slices fresh pineapple
1 cup sliced fresh strawberries
1 fresh mango, sliced, for garnish

In the top of a double boiler, prepare the custard by combining the egg yolks, the 1/4 cup sugar, and salt. Beat with a wire whisk until pale and creamy. In a medium saucepan combine the milk with 1 cup of the whipping cream and bring to a boil over medium-high heat. Slowly pour into the egg mixture, stirring constantly.

Set the double boiler over hot but not boiling water and cook, stirring constantly, until the mixture thickens lightly and just coats a metal spoon. Remove from the heat and stir in 2 tablespoons of the rum. Allow to cool.

Slice the cake in half crosswise and place the bottom half in a 9-inch-diameter serving bowl. Sprinkle the cake with 1/4 cup of the rum, then cover with the sliced pineapple. Set the top half of the cake on the pineapple. Sprinkle with 1/4 cup of the rum and cover with the custard. Seal with plastic wrap and refrigerate for 3 to 4 hours.

To serve, whip the remaining 1 cup cream in a chilled medium bowl until stiff peaks form. Beat in the 2 tablespoons sugar and the final 1 tablespoon rum. Cover the surface of the custard with the whipped cream, smoothing with a rubber spatula. Decorate with mango slices and serve.

Yield: 8 to 10 servings.

# Banana Whip

$\mathcal{T}$his recipe, with its tropical fruit cream, was first encountered on the English isle of Anguilla. It turns up, however, in virtually every British or once-British corner of the Caribbean.

## Fruit Whip
4 large bananas
1/4 cup sugar, or to taste
1/2 cup orange juice
1/4 cup light rum
3 egg whites
1/8 teaspoon salt

## Fruit Cream
4 egg yolks
3 tablespoons sugar
1 cup orange juice (see Note)

In a large bowl mash the bananas with the sugar, orange juice, and rum. Taste and add more sugar if desired. In a medium bowl beat the egg whites with the salt until stiff peaks form, then fold lightly but thoroughly into the banana mixture. Chill until lightly set, 3 to 4 hours.

Prepare the Fruit Cream by beating the egg yolks with the sugar until pale yellow. Transfer to a heavy saucepan, add the orange juice, and cook over low heat, beating constantly with a wire whisk until the mixture starts to foam. Remove from the heat immediately—the mixture must not be allowed to boil. Chill thoroughly for 3 to 4 hours.

To serve, spoon the Fruit Cream over the banana mixture or serve on the side.

Yield: 6 servings.

Note: You can vary the flavor dramatically by using different tropical fruit juices in the cream. Vary the amount of sugar as needed, from fruit to fruit.

# Daiquiri Soufflé

From its freshly squeezed lime juice to its spiking with light rum, this cold soufflé will always speak to you of the Caribbean—as does the cocktail from which it takes its name.

1 envelope (1/4 oz) unflavored gelatin
1 cup milk
3/4 cup sugar
4 eggs, separated
1/4 teaspoon allspice
2 tablespoons freshly squeezed lime juice
1 tablespoon light rum
1 cup whipping cream
1 teaspoon grated lime zest
1 teaspoon grated lemon zest

Prepare a 4-cup soufflé dish by wrapping a strip of double-thickness aluminum foil 3 inches wide by 22 inches long around to extend 1 1/2 inches above the rim. Fasten with tape and set the dish aside.

In a small saucepan combine the gelatin with the milk and let stand 1 minute to soften. Stir in 1/2 cup of the sugar and cook over medium heat, stirring constantly, until the gelatin and sugar dissolve. Beat the egg yolks in a bowl, then quickly whisk in some of the hot milk mixture. Stir the egg yolk mixture into the saucepan.

Add the allspice and cook, stirring constantly, until the custard thickens, about 2 minutes. Remove from the heat, then stir in the lime juice and rum. Transfer to a large bowl and chill until the mixture mounds on a spoon.

In a separate bowl beat the egg whites until they are foamy, then gradually add the remaining 1/4 cup sugar. Beat until stiff but not dry. In a chilled medium bowl, beat the cream until stiff, then fold both it and the beaten egg whites into the chilled gelatin mixture. Spoon into the prepared soufflé dish and garnish with lime and lemon zest. Refrigerate until firm, about 3 hours. Remove the foil collar when ready to serve.

Yield: 6 to 8 servings.

# Rum–Raisin Soufflé

Chopped raisins make all the difference in this cold soufflé from Barbados, joining forces with an old friend in the dark rum. You can use the directions in the above recipe to prepare the soufflé dish.

1 1/2 teaspoons cornstarch
3 tablespoons plus 1/3 cup water
1 cup evaporated milk
5 eggs, separated
3/4 cup confectioners' sugar
1 1/2 envelopes (1 1/2 tablespoons) unflavored gelatin
1 teaspoon vanilla extract
1/2 cup dark rum
3 tablespoons chopped raisins
1/8 teaspoon salt

Dissolve the cornstarch in the 3 tablespoons water, then transfer to a large saucepan and stir in the evaporated milk. Warm over low heat until the mixture thickens, then remove from the heat.

In a medium bowl beat the egg yolks with the confectioners' sugar until thick and pale yellow. Dissolve the gelatin in the 1/3 cup water. Stir the dissolved gelatin and the egg yolk mixture into the mixture in the saucepan.

Stir over low heat for 5 minutes, then stir in the vanilla, rum, and raisins. Remove from the heat. In a large bowl beat the egg whites with the salt until stiff. Stir half the beaten whites into the saucepan, then fold in the remainder very gently. Pour into the prepared soufflé dish and chill until set, about 2 hours. Remove the foil collar when ready to serve.

Yield: 8 servings.

# Coffee Bombe

Between its coffee ice cream and its coffee-flavored liqueur, this icy wonder of classical European origin is designed for those who can't get enough of one of the Caribbean's favorite flavors.

1 quart coffee ice cream
1 pint French vanilla ice cream
1/2 cup chopped toasted cashew nuts
Whipped cream, for topping
Coffee bean candies, for garnish
Tia Maria or other coffee-flavored liqueur, for sprinkling

Chill a large metal mixing bowl or bombe mold in the freezer overnight. Reserve 1 cup of the coffee ice cream for the top of the bombe, then allow the rest to soften. Spread the softened ice cream around the bottom and sides of the bowl. Freeze until firm.

Combine the vanilla ice cream with the chopped cashews and pack into the middle of the chilled bowl, stopping about 1 inch from the top. Let the reserved 1 cup coffee ice cream soften and use to top the vanilla ice cream. Cover with plastic wrap and return to the freezer until it's time to serve.

Invert the bombe onto a serving platter and remove the bowl. Decorate with the whipped cream and coffee bean candies. Srinkle each slice with the coffee liqueur as it is served.

Yield: 10 servings.

# Island Parfaits

The French word for "perfect" is "parfait," and it is applied with good reason to this layered chilled dessert. Although of course you can combine the tropical fruits of your choice, I've found this particular blend a winner time after time. And the grated coconut provides the perfect finish.

1/2 large fresh pineapple, peeled, cored, and cubed
2 fresh papayas, peeled, seeded, and cubed
1 fresh mango, peeled, pitted, and chopped
1 large banana
1/2 cup freshly squeezed orange juice
1/2 cup grated unsweetened coconut, for sprinkling

In a large bowl combine the pineapple, papaya, and mango. Combine the banana with the orange juice in a food processor or blender, processing until smooth. Fill tall dessert glasses halfway with the fruit, then top with the banana mixture. Stir just enough to mix.

Cover the glasses with plastic wrap and chill several hours so the flavors can blend. Just before serving, sprinkle the top of each parfait with the grated coconut.

Yield: 6 servings.

# Papaya Delight

This molded dessert can be accented with strawberries or cherries—even with a colorful mixture of preserved fruits. But for the sweet taste of the islands, leave the job to ripe papaya.

3/4 cup sugar
1 cup water
1 envelope (1/4 oz) unflavored gelatin
1 tablespoon lemon juice
1 cup fresh papaya pulp
2 egg whites
Whipped cream, for topping

In a large saucepan combine the sugar with 3/4 cup of the water and cook over low heat, stirring constantly, until the sugar is dissolved. Add the gelatin to the remaining 1/4 cup water and let it soften, then stir it into the syrup. Let the mixture cool.

In a small bowl combine the lemon juice and papaya pulp. Add to the syrup and beat thoroughly. Chill until thick. Beat the egg whites until stiff, then fold them gently into the papaya mixture. Pour into a 9-inch decorative mold or serving bowl. Chill until set, about 2 hours. Serve with whipped cream.

Yield: 6 to 8 servings.

# Pineapple Royal

$\mathcal{P}$ineapple may be the main ingredient here as well as the eye-catching delivery system, yet I think the word royal says it all about this dessert. It may well prove the conversation piece of your Caribbean dinner.

6 small fresh pineapples
1 pint vanilla ice cream, softened
1 cup whipping cream, whipped
3 tablespoons light rum
1/2 teaspoon ground mace
1/4 teaspoon grated fresh ginger
1/2 cup diced banana
1/2 cup diced orange sections
1/2 cup sliced fresh strawberries

Slice off the tops of the pineapples, wrap the tops in aluminum foil, and chill them in the freezer. Scoop out the pineapple pulp, leaving shells about 1/2 inch thick. Wrap the shells and chill with the tops. In a large bowl combine the pineapple pulp with the remaining ingredients.

Fill the pineapple shells with the fruit mixture and return to the freezer until the filling is firm, at least 1 hour. When ready to serve, set each of the filled shells on a dessert plate and set a pineapple top on each.

Yield: 6 servings.

# Passion Fruit Mousse

*T*he mousse is yet another of those classic European dessert forms that has found fresh life in the Caribbean. It seems that every cook has a favorite recipe, using his or her favorite fruit growing right outside the kitchen window. This delight showcasing passion fruit is something I first tasted along the north coast of Puerto Rico.

6 eggs, separated
1/2 cup sugar
3 tablespoons cornstarch
2 cups passion fruit juice
1 envelope (1/4 oz) unflavored gelatin
1/4 cup water
1/8 teaspoon salt
1 cup whipping cream
Fresh mint leaves, for garnish

In a large bowl beat the egg yolks with the sugar until they form a pale yellow ribbon. Dissolve the cornstarch in the passion fruit juice, then add to the yolk mixture. Cook in the top of a double boiler until the liquid thickens enough to coat a spoon. Set aside to cool.

Dissolve the gelatin in the water and add to the mixture. In a separate bowl beat the egg whites with the salt until stiff. Fold into the egg mixture and refrigerate until just beginning to set. Beat the cream until stiff, then fold it in as well. Chill the mousse until firm. Garnish with fresh mint leaves and serve.

Yield: 8 servings.

# Martinique Coffee Mousse

Many islands in the Caribbean have traditions of coffee growing—all descendants of the single plant that Gabriel Mathieu de Clieu nursed with his own water ration on the perilous voyage from France to Martinique in the early 1700s. I've named this lush (and very French) coffee mousse after the island that was the first place to cultivate coffee in the New World.

4 eggs, separated
1/2 cup sugar
1/2 cup strong brewed coffee
2 tablespoons Tia Maria or other coffee-flavored liqueur
2 teaspoons unflavored gelatin
Shaved chocolate, for garnish
Whipped cream, for topping

In a medium bowl beat the egg yolks with the sugar until pale and fluffy; set aside. Mix the coffee and the liqueur in a small saucepan, sprinkle with the gelatin, and set aside for 5 minutes to soften, then cook over medium heat, stirring constantly, just until the gelatin dissolves. Let cool a bit.

Add the cooled gelatin mixture to the reserved egg yolks, stirring constantly. Let cool completely. In a medium bowl beat the egg whites until they are stiff but not dry and fold them into the mousse. Spoon into individual dessert dishes and chill in the refrigerator. Garnish with shaved chocolate and whipped cream before serving.

Yield: 6 servings.

# Mousse à l'Ananas

Also from the French West Indies comes this most famed of Caribbean mousses, one that celebrates the exploding sweetness of ripe pineapple not only in the mousse itself but in the custard sauce served alongside it.

## Mousse
2 cups unsweetened pineapple juice
1 cup sugar
6 tablespoons cornstarch
6 egg whites
1/8 teaspoon salt

## Custard Sauce
6 egg yolks
1/4 cup sugar
1/8 teaspoon salt
2 cups half-and-half
1 teaspoon vanilla extract
1 cup coarsely chopped fresh pineapple

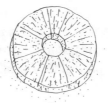

Pour the pineapple juice into a large saucepan and add the sugar. Dissolve the cornstarch in a little of the juice, then add it to the pan. Stir with a wooden spoon over low heat for 5 minutes. Remove from the heat and let the mixture cool.

In a large bowl beat the egg whites with the salt until stiff peaks form. Fold gently but thoroughly into the juice mixture. Transfer the mousse to a serving dish and chill in the refrigerator.

Prepare the sauce by beating the egg yolks, sugar, and salt together in the top of a double boiler away from the heat. Beat until the mixture forms a pale yellow ribbon. Scald the half-and-half in a separate saucepan, then pour it slowly into the egg yolk mixture, stirring constantly with a wooden spoon or wire whisk.

Pour hot but not boiling water into the bottom part of the double boiler, replace the top pan containing the yolk mixture, and cook over very low heat until the mixture thickens enough to coat a spoon, stirring constantly. Remove from the heat and stir until slightly cooled. Strain the sauce, then add the vanilla extract and chopped pineapple. Chill in a serving bowl and serve alongside the pineapple mousse.

Yield: 6 to 8 servings.

It's doubtful that any other region on earth produces the variety of tropical fruits the Caribbean does. A few treasures are native, but most—including the mango, orange, and lime—were introduced by settlers won over by the rich soil and climate. Still other fruits are the result of spontaneous crossbreeding and go by names that tend to show it: the tangelo, the tangor, and, best of all, the ugli.

# Nutmeg Ice Cream

*I* can never make this ice cream without remembering Grenada—and the young island boy who (for a price, of course) took me, my wife, and my children in his little boat from the colorful harbor at St. George's to the idyllic stretch of beach called Grand Anse. It was quite a boat ride, and this is quite an ice cream!

2 cups milk
1 cup half-and-half
4 large eggs
3/4 cup sugar
3/4 cup sweetened condensed milk
2 medium-sized whole nutmegs, freshly grated
1 1/2 cups whipping cream

In a large saucepan over low heat, warm the milk with the half-and-half. Heat only to the point at which steam rises from the surface—do not boil. Meanwhile, in a medium bowl thoroughly blend the eggs and sugar. Whisk a small amount of the hot milk mixture into the eggs, then pour this into the saucepan.

Stirring constantly, cook over low heat until the mixture thickens into a custard. Again, do not boil. Remove the pan from the heat and stir in the condensed milk and nutmeg. Let cool to room temperature. Stir in the whipping cream and refrigerate for at least 2 hours. Freeze in a half-gallon ice cream maker according to the manufacturer's instructions. Serve chilled.

Yield: 8 servings.

# Coffees & Other Beverages

hy yes, this final chapter does have a lot to do with rum. Yet it stops short of being the drink chapter that seems de rigeur at the end of every Caribbean cookbook. I'd love to give you one, of course, since some of my best friends are Caribbean rum drinks. But this is a dessert cookbook, after all. So I think any drink included here should be something that adds a special glow to the close of a meal, not just something that puts extra zing into a day at the beach. This doesn't change the fact that drinking three pina coladas in Puerto Rico is like eating three desserts, but that's only one of many facts I can't change.

Over the years, the confluence of great local coffee and great local rum has produced—you guessed it!—great coffee rum drinks. Every island has several that are a lot like every other island's, which means you'll be told with each that you can get it nowhere else. Indeed, every resort worth its fitness center has a list of coffees and other beverages ostensibly its alone. What I've pulled together here is a clear-eyed synthesis, a brief collection that points the way toward terrific flavor while leaving you free to experiment.

Being me, I couldn't quit without slipping in a few drinks for exoticism. Waiting just beyond the familiar world of spiked flaming coffees are such wonders as the Caribbean eggnog known as coquito, a beer made with fresh ginger, and a holiday specialty concocted from the dried petals of sorrel—just when you thought it was safe to order another Bahama Mama!

# Café Aruba

Aruba, sister island to the one that gives the world Curacao, offers us this festive dessert coffee flavored with orange and crowned with whipped cream.

3 cups strong brewed coffee
Zest of 1/4 orange, julienned
1 orange, peeled and sliced
1 tablespoon sugar
1 teaspoon bitters
1/2 cup whipping cream, whipped

Measure the hot coffee into a glass pot, then add the orange zest and slices. Steep over low heat for about 15 minutes. Add the sugar and bitters. Do not boil. Strain and pour into 4 or 5 warmed heatproof glasses. Top with whipped cream and serve at once.
Yield: 4 to 5 servings.

# Jamaican Coffee

Jamaicans not only love the coffee they grow in the Blue Mountains, they love the liqueur that's made from at least some of it. It's important, then, that this book feature at least one specialty coffee enlivened by Tia Maria.

6 cups hot brewed coffee
3/4 cup Tia Maria liqueur
Sugar, to taste

Fill 6 warmed cups three-fourths full of hot coffee, then top with Tia Maria. Sweeten lightly with sugar to taste and serve.
Yield: 6 servings.

# Coffee Grog

Grog is a word with special meaning in the Caribbean. Bajans grin "Let's fire a grog" as an invitation to a drink. In this recipe, which hails from Barbados, the spirit of the buccaneers still lives in the rum and spices that were their island stock-in-trade.

1/3 cup packed brown sugar
1 tablespoon unsalted butter
1/8 teaspoon ground cinnamon
1/8 teaspoon freshly grated nutmeg
1/8 teaspoon ground cloves
1/8 teaspoon ground allspice
4 1/2 cups hot brewed coffee
3/4 cup dark rum
3/4 cup half-and-half
6 twists of orange zest

In a medium bowl cream together the brown sugar and butter, then thoroughly blend in all the spices. Add the coffee, rum, and half-and-half. Blend well. Ladle into 6 warmed coffee mugs, garnish with the twists of orange zest, and serve immediately.

Yield: 6 servings.

# Cancun Café

As we've already seen, the Mexican Caribbean adds to the islands its own love affair of coffee paired with native chocolate. In the case of this refreshing drink, just about every ingredient makes the union that much stronger.

1 cup strong brewed coffee, chilled
1 cup coffee ice cream
1/4 cup coffee-flavored liqueur
2 tablespoons creme de cacao
Shaved chocolate, for garnish

In a blender container combine the coffee, ice cream, coffee liqueur, and creme de cacao. Cover and blend until smooth. Pour into 4 champagne glasses, garnish with shaved chocolate, and serve.

Yield: 4 servings.

# Flaming Rum Coffee

You don't need a whole array of ingredients to end a meal with theatrical flair, as any islander will assure you. This three-ingredient wonder is about as simple as its gets.

6 teaspoons sugar
3 1/2 cups hot brewed coffee
6 tablespoons rum

Into each of 6 demitasse cups, measure 1 teaspoon sugar, then fill three-fourths full with the hot coffee. Float 1 tablespoon rum atop the coffee in each cup and ignite carefully with a long-stemmed match. When the flame has burned out, stir the coffee, rum, and sugar together and serve at once.

Yield: 6 servings.

# Hot Buttered Rum

You can bet that on those rare occasions when the weather turns cool—and I can attest it doesn't take much to make people shiver in the Caribbean—all hands reach for a bit of pirate tradition in this hot and buttery rum. I can also attest that it warms more than the hands!

1 stick cinnamon
1/4 cup light rum
1/2 teaspoon unsalted butter
3/4 cup apple juice or cider, heated
Freshly grated nutmeg, for sprinkling

Set the cinnamon stick in an 8-ounce mug, then add the rum and the butter. Pour in the hot cider and stir. Grate a little nutmeg on top and serve warm.
Yield: 1 drink.

# Batido Cubano

Cubans have always loved what happens when you take a blender to the very freshest fruit and pour out a refreshing drink. The result is known as a refresco de papaya or whatever fruit is in favor at the moment. Colloquially, it's called a batido.

1/2 cup light rum
2/3 cup coarsely chopped fresh papaya
Confectioners' sugar, to taste
1/2 cup finely crushed ice
1 sprig fresh mint

Combine the rum with the papaya in an electric blender and blend on high speed until the fruit is pulverized. Taste and blend in a little confectioners' sugar, if desired. Place the ice in a goblet and pour in the drink. Stir to mix. Garnish with a mint sprig and serve.
Yield: 1 drink.

# Coquito

*Y*es, there is eggnog for the holidays in the Caribbean, but it's likely to taste quite different from any you've sipped anywhere else. This version, known as coquito in its native Puerto Rico, is a pretty good summary of what flavors island-ers think of when it's time for "eggnog" in the tropics.

4 egg yolks
1 can (15 oz) sweetened coconut cream
1 can (14 oz) sweetened condensed milk
1 1/2 cups half-and-half
1 bottle (750 ml) light rum
Ground cinnamon, for sprinkling

In a large punch bowl whisk together the egg yolks, cream of coconut, condensed milk, and half-and-half. Cover and refrigerate for several hours. Just before serving, stir again and sprinkle with cinnamon.

Yield: 25 servings.

*It's hard to imagine a tropical fruit more generous than the cashew. Most trees bear either fruit or nuts—the cashew bears both. The bright red fruity part of the cashew is sometimes called the cashew apple. Although it is sometimes eaten raw or stewed, it is usually made into jelly, wine, or liqueur. Cashew nuts, once separated from the ripened pedacles, are shelled and roasted until they achieve crispness and the familiar tan color. Perhaps the only ungenerous aspect of the cashew tree is that it's related botanically to poison ivy. There's a part of its nutshell which can produce a rash.*

# Sorrel Drink

Sorrel, also called rosella or hibiscus sabdariffa, is a tropical plant whose red petals are popular in drinks, jams, and jellies. Though the petals are sold fresh in the Caribbean at Christmastime, they are available dried all year in 2-ounce packages. This lovely pink holiday drink is sorrel's pride and joy. Remember to allow 4 to 5 days for the petals to steep.

3 dozen fresh or 1 ounce dried sorrel (rosella) petals
1 stick cinnamon
1 large piece dried orange zest
6 whole cloves
2 cups sugar
8 cups boiling water
1/2 cup medium dark rum
1 teaspoon ground cinnamon
1/4 teaspoon ground cloves

In a large jar or crock, combine the sorrel petals, cinnamon stick, orange zest, whole cloves, and sugar. Pour in the boiling water. Cover loosely and set aside at room temperature for 2 to 3 days.

Strain, then add the ground cinnamon and cloves. Set aside for an additional 2 days. Strain through a fine sieve lined with cheesecloth. Serve in chilled glasses, with ice cubes if desired.

Yield: 2 quarts.

# Ginger Beer

The making of this pungent homebrew has a history just about as old as the Caribbean, all leading up to popularity today as a commercial product. Most islanders still make their own, however, giving the brew extra flavor and body by adding "chewstick" (a climbing vine listed officially as Gouania lupuloides) bought in bundles at island markets. You'll be quite satisfied with this ginger beer even without the benefit of chewstick.

1 tablespoon grated fresh ginger
1/3 cup lime juice
Zest of 1 lime
1 cup sugar
4 cups boiling water
1 teaspoon active dry yeast
1/4 cup lukewarm water

In a large bowl combine the ginger, lime juice, zest, and sugar. Pour in the boiling water. In a small bowl sprinkle the yeast over the lukewarm water. Let stand for 5 minutes, then stir to dissolve. Let the dissolved yeast stand in a warm place until it begins to bubble, about 5 minutes more. Stir it into the ginger mixture.

Cover the bowl and leave in a warm, draft-free place for 1 week, stirring every other day. Strain through a fine sieve. Bottle and let stand at room temperature for 3 to 4 more days. Chill and serve in tumblers, with ice cubes if desired.

Yield: 1 quart.

# Sources of Caribbean Foods

*I*n addition to countless bodegas, fresh produce stands, and specialty foods stores that stock Caribbean foods, many chain supermarkets stock Caribbean foods. Look for Goya-brand foods for high-quality canned and packaged Caribbean food products.

The following list includes businesses that sell fresh and packaged Caribbean foods in some areas of the United States and Canada. If no business is listed for your city, a phone call to the nearest listed business may provide you with information on how to find foods closer to home.

## ❀ California

**Caribbean Delites**
1057 E. Artesia Blvd.
Long Beach, CA 90805
(213) 422-5594

**Frieda's Finest Produce Specialties**
P.O. Box 58488
Los Angeles, CA 90058
(213) 627-2981 (CA)
(800) 421-2981 (outside CA)
Exotic fruits and vegetables. Available by mail order and for retail distribution.

**La Preferida, Inc.**
4615 Alameda ST.
Los Angeles, CA 90056
(213) 232-4322
Contact:Ivan Bayona

**Rosado's International Foods, Inc.**
1711 Little Orchard, Ste. B
San Jose, CA 95125
(408) 298-2326

## ❀ Florida

**Goya**
1900 N.W. 92nd Ave.
Miami, FL 33172
(305) 592-3150

**Jamaica Groceries & Spices**
9628 S.W. 160th St.
Colonial Shopping Centre
Miami, FL 33157
(305) 252-1197

**J. R. Brooks and Son, Inc.**
P.O. Drawer 9
18400 SW 256th St.
Homestead, FL 33090-0009
(800) 423-4808 (FL)
(800) 327-4833 (outside FL)
(800) 338-1022 (Canada)
Tropical fruits.

**La Preferida, Inc. (Florida)**
9108 N.W. 105th Way
Medley, FL 33178
(305) 883-8444
Contact: Carlos Bordon

**McDonald Import Co., Inc.**
300 N. Chrome Ave.
Florida City, FL 33034
*or*
P.O. Box 970134
Miami, FL 33197
(305) 246-1816

**Temptations — Caribbean Harvest**
P.O. Box 170105
Miami, FL 33017
Contact: Jackie Shepard

West Indian Food
Specialties
6035 Miramar Parkway
Miramar, FL 33023
(305) 962-6418

## ❀ Georgia

Dekalb World Farmers Market
3000 E. Ponce de Leon
Decatur, GA 30034
(404) 377-6401
A wonderful source of foods from
around the world.

Dewars Fine Foods
1937 Peachtree Road
Atlanta, GA 30309
(404) 351-3663

## ❀ Illinois

La Preferida, Inc. (Chicago)
3400 W. 35th St.
Chicago, IL 60632
(312) 254-7200
Contact: William L. Steinberth,
or Robert Gouwens

## ❀ New Jersey

Goya Foods
100 Seaview Drive
Secaucus, NJ 07094
(201) 348-4900

## ❀ New York

Casa Hispania International
Food Market
PO Box 587
73 Poningo St.
Port Chester, NY 10578
(914) 939-9333

Dean & Deluca
560 Broadway, Suite 304
New York, NY 10012
(800) 221-7714 (except NY)
(800) 431-1691 (NY)
Call or write for a free catalog; they sell a
variety of imported and domestic specialty
foods.

Tropica Island Traders
170 Fifth Ave. and Twenty Second St.
New York, NY 10010
(212) 627-0808
Specializing in products from the Caribbean.

## ❀ Texas

La Preferida, Inc. (Texas)
4000 Telephone Rd.
Houston, TX 77087
(713) 643-7128
Contact: Edgar Martinez

## ❀ Washington, D.C.

Continental Trading Co.
7826 Easter Ave., N.W.
Suite 500
Washington, D.C.
(202) 829-5620

## ❀ Canada

Toronto Caribbean Corner
57 Kensington Ave.
Toronto, Ont.
(416) 593-0008

Tropical Harvest Food Market
57 Kensington Ave.
Toronto, Ont.
(416) 593-9279

West Indian Fine Foods
Terrace Brae Plaza
Markham & Lawrence
Scarborough, Ont.
(416) 431-9353

# Index

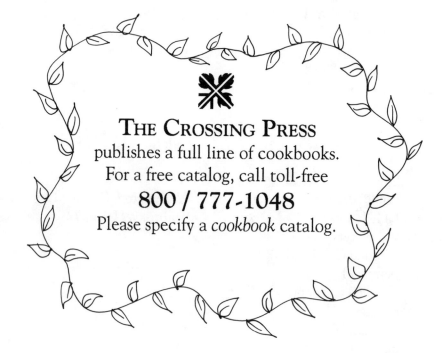